W9-BYG-242

ALWAYS READY
TODAY'S U.S. COAST GUARD

KIT & CAROLYN BONNER

MBI

This edition first published in 2004 by
MBI Publishing Company, Galtier Plaza,
Suite 200, 380 Jackson Street, St. Paul, MN
55101-3885 USA

© Kit and Carolyn Bonner, 2004

All rights reserved. With the exception of
quoting brief passages for the purposes of review,
no part of this publication may be reproduced
without prior written permission from the
Publisher.

The information in this book is true and complete
to the best of our knowledge. All
recommendations are made without any guarantee
on the part of the author or Publisher, who also
disclaim any liability incurred in connection with
the use of this data or specific details.

We recognize that some words, model names and
designations, for example, mentioned herein are
the property of the trademark holder. We use
them for identification purposes only. This is not
an official publication.

MBI Publishing Company titles are also available
at discounts in bulk quantity for industrial or
sales-promotional use. For details write to
Special Sales Manager at Motorbooks
International Wholesalers & Distributors,
Galtier Plaza, Suite 200, 380 Jackson Street,
St. Paul, MN 55101-3885 USA.

ISBN 0-7603-1727-5

Edited by Amy Glaser
Designed by Mandy Iverson

Printed in China

On the front cover: The high-endurance cutter
Gallatin (WHEC-721) operates with an over-the-
horizon, high-speed craft and an MH-90 Enforcer
helicopter. The high-speed boats and helicopter
are designed to catch and seize illegal drug
carrying go-fast boats. *USCG*

On the frontispiece: A crewman aboard a C-130
Hercules is about to throw a smoke bomb out of
the craft to mark the locationwhere a survival
package will be aimed during this practice run.
The object is to hit on or near the smoke bomb
to simulate a rescue attempt. *Author's collection,
Mary Mesmer*

On the title page: The high endurance cutter
Boutwell (WHEC-719) is in the North Arabian Gulf
on May 6, 2003, to provide fuel, food, laundry,
and showers to the crew of the Island class patrol
tied to her starboard aft side. *USCG*

On the back cover 1: On April 20, 2003, a
boarding term team from the cutter Boutwell has
just examined the craft in the background and
will search for contraband and dangers to
coalition forces elsewhere. *USCG*

On the back cover 2: The *Island*-class patrol boat
Monhegan returns from a drug interdiction on
April 26, 2003, with over 2,000 pounds of
marijuana and three smugglers. So far, the
Monhegan has successfully carried out eight anti-
drug missions. *USCG*

Author Bio: Kit and Carolyn Bonner are naval
historians and photographers. They have
authored *Great Ship Disasters*, *Warship Boneyards*,
Cold War at Sea, and *Great Naval Disasters*. Kit
was the naval consultant for the 1997 film,
Titanic. They live in Ione, California.

Contents

Dedication

This book is dedicated to all of the past, present, and future men and women of the U.S. Coast Guard. When they say, "Take my hand, and I promise I will not let you go," they mean it—even at the risk of their own lives. This book further recognizes the crews of the *Boutwell*, *Walnut*, *Island*-class patrol boats, and Port Security Units; Ernie Bodai, M.D.; and Frank Spinelli a rare man of integrity and a good friend for many years.

Foreword

Over the last two centuries, the United States has evolved from a group of separate and distinct states into one of the most powerful nations in the world. As our country developed, the Coast Guard evolved with it, from a small contingent of Revenue Cutters to lifesavers, law-enforcement agents, protectors of the environment, and war fighters. No matter what role we filled over the last 213 years, one thing has remained constant: Our people have willingly risked their own lives for their country and their fellow men and women. I can think of nothing more noble or courageous.

Our missions are many and varied. Among them are search and rescue, marine safety, environmental protection, drug interdiction, migrant interdiction, fisheries enforcement, aids to navigation, and domestic and polar icebreaking. While homeland security has understandably garnered more attention as of late, the Coast Guard has always played a significant role in that area.

The U.S. Coast Guard is also a military organization, which has served proudly and with distinction in every war and military conflict since its inception.

Today, our service is made up of 93,000 active duty, reserve, civilian, and auxiliary members. It is these people, past and present, who have truly made the Coast Guard an organization recognized around the globe as the world's premier maritime service. During my 39-year Coast Guard career, I have personally witnessed the dedication and commitment that our people have put into every task and mission. They are the heart and soul of our service. They embody our core values of honor, respect, and devotion to duty. I am truly proud to be associated with every one.

As we have from our beginning, the U.S. Coast Guard continues to fulfill its motto of being *Semper Paratus*—Always Ready—to protect America's safety, security, environment, and commerce.

—Admiral Thomas H. Collins

Introduction

The Shield of Freedom

All Coast Guard personnel are considered part of the shield of freedom. This means that they stand between the average citizen and harm that may come from the sea to the shores of the United States and its protectorates. The shield of freedom includes over 40,000 men and women who have chosen to become Coasties. All can aspire to become a four-star admiral, like Admiral Thomas H. Collins, who serves as the commandant of this small, but highly significant, maritime force.

Admiral Collins follows in the wake of many before him who have met challenge after challenge, ranging from hordes of illegal Cuban migrants in the 1980s to fighting Imperial Germany's U-boats in World War I. Admiral Collins is the only four-star admiral in the Coast Guard and reports to Tom Ridge, Homeland Security secretary, who heads the recently created Department of Homeland Security, a Cabinet-level position.

Events and needs

The Coast Guard is primarily driven by civil and military events. As an organization, it does not remain static or rest on yesterday's achievements for its identity. That identity changes with the needs of the nation.

An explosion aboard the SS *Pulaski* in 1838 demonstrated that regulations were needed to reduce the number of deaths from improper steamboat operations. It was not

Admiral Thomas Collins is gratified that the public recognizes the value of the U.S. Coast Guard. Admiral Collins has served on a number of ships and shore stations and has worked his way up to the top post in the nation's primary maritime safety force. *USCG*

long before the Steamboat Inspection Service was inaugurated. Rather than bury it within the overburdened Revenue Cutter Service, a shore installation was created, and regulations were written and enforced.

The damage and loss of vessels from collisions with icebergs in the North Atlantic, such as the sinking of the RMS *Titanic* in April 1912, prompted the creation of the United States-led International Ice Patrol.

An explosion on the SS *Mont Blanc* in Halifax Harbor, Canada, claimed hundreds of lives in June 1917 and laid to rest an entire town and port. The U.S. Congress reacted by giving the Coast Guard the task to control shipping in U.S. ports to ensure a higher degree of safety. In the wake of the terrorist attacks in September 2001, the Coast Guard has been granted wider powers and more equipment to further protect shipping portals to the United States.

In September 1934 the cruise ship SS *Morro Castle* burned in full view of thousands of onlookers off the beach in Asbury Park, New Jersey. Of the total crew and passengers, 124 perished. Few lifeboats were launched and many passengers had to fend for themselves. Many more would have died had it not been for the Coast Guard, but new regulations for safety at sea were still needed.

The Coast Guard has always had the collateral, yet mandatory, obligation to first obey the law of the sea by saving the lives of others. In 1979, it performed the Mariel boatlift, one of the most extensive search-and-rescue (SAR) operations in the history of the United States. Cuban dictator Fidel Castro allowed anyone to leave Cuba via the small port in Mariel, Cuba. The migrants exited in everything that could or would float, and many had to be rescued by the Coast Guard and U.S. Navy. This further reinforced the role of saving lives at sea.

Encouraging Diversity

The Coast Guard and its predecessors have been on the leading edge of encouraging diversity by offering opportunities and responsibilities to minorities and women. The Coast Guard ensures that the civil and military duties under its jurisdiction are honorably fulfilled, and its leadership has earned a reputation for humanitarianism and doing the right thing.

For example, Ida Lewis-Wilson saved a total of 18 lives during her tenure as the keeper of the Lime Rock Lighthouse. From 1828 through 1947 about 138 women have served as lighthouse keepers. Lewis-Wilson was awarded a Gold Life Saving Medal on July 16, 1881, for saving two soldiers who fell through the ice on February 4, 1881.

Barbara Mabrity and her husband, Michael, were keepers of the Key West Lighthouse from 1826 until 1864. Michael died just six years after they took up their charge. Barbara shepherded the station through storms and hurricanes and saved countless lives until she was 82-years-old. Mabrity's family followed her service as keepers until 1915 when the lighthouse was automated.

Captain Richard Etheridge was appointed as the keeper of the Pea Island Life Saving Station on January 24, 1880. He and many of his surf men were African-American and quickly

The 110-foot *Island* class patrol boat *Adak* and its crew provide port security in New York harbor and over the Statue of Liberty on August 22, 2002. The *Adak* is based in Sandy Hook, New Jersey, and was deployed in Operation Iraqi Freedom. *USCG*

earned an excellent reputation for running one of the best stations on the Carolina coast. The area was known for its dangerous weather, shipwrecks, and casualties, and Etheridge and his crew rescued many lives at great peril to themselves. Yet their efforts went formally unnoticed until March 5, 1996. Richard Etheridge and six of his African-American crew were posthumously awarded the Gold Life Saving Medal for heroism. Etheridge died while trying to save a person's life on May 8,

1900—96 years before he was recognized for his heroism, but he and his men did finally receive the recognition they deserved.

Lieutenant Colleen A. Cain, USCG Rotary Wing Aviator, was the Coast Guard's third female aviator and the service's first helicopter pilot. She achieved this title in June 1979, and was ultimately rated as an aircraft commander. In the predawn hours of January 7, 1982, while assigned at Air Station Barbers Point, Hawaii, severe weather did not stop Lieutenant Cain and her crew from taking off on a rescue mission aboard a HH-52A Sea Guard helicopter. The rescue helicopter never made contact with the crew of the sinking fishing boat because the aircraft struck the side of a mountain killing the entire crew instantly. In her memory, the Coast Guard dedicated Cain Hall at the Reserve Training Center in Yorktown, Pennsylvania.

These Coast Guard personnel and their predecessors are just a small number of those who willingly sacrifice all to save others.

Becoming Part of The U.S. Coast Guard

The Coast Guard of the twenty-first century uses the whole-person concept in recruiting, and recruiters have little difficulty selecting some of the best and brightest that this nation has to offer. To enter through the "hawse pipe" or via enlistment, a person must be between the ages of 17 and 27, but there are exceptions up to age 36 for those with prior military service or specialized skills that the Coast Guard would need. An applicant must have a high school diploma or GED. A medical exam is required, and those with asthma are excluded due to safety concerns. Applicants must have high moral character with no felonies on their record, including drug abuse. Those with a history of domestic violence are excluded since the USCG is a law enforcement agency. Candidates must also pass a written aptitude test. Once candidates have success-fully completed all entrance requirements, they can be sworn in to the U.S. Coast Guard and sent to Cape May, New Jersey, for recruit training. Further specialty training is offered at other locations, such as Petaluma, California. Some recruit camp graduates opt to go directly

to sea as part of a deck force, and others plan ahead for promotion to senior enlisted, warrant officer, or officer candidate school.

It took until 1949 for the U.S. government to recognize that members of the Coast Guard should be compensated at the same pay level with the same pay grades as other services in the Department of Defense. The Career Compensation Act of 1949 was passed into law, and Coast Guard enlisted ratings became comparable to those of the U.S. Navy, Army, Marine Corps, and Air Force with the "E" series. E-1 is a seaman recruit, and E-10 is the master chief petty officer of the Coast Guard, the highest enlisted rating.

Coast Guard officers can come up through the ranks or go through officer candidate school. The Maritime Academies also graduate officers in the Merchant Marines that could be reserve officers in the Coast Guard, but most go through the U.S. Coast Guard Academy in New London, Connecticut, which graduates approx-imately 175 ensigns each year. Generally, these ensigns are introduced to the fleet aboard a cutter and must serve for a minimum of five years. The first two years spent aboard a cutter teach the practical aspects of being a Coast Guard leader, and, as with the Navy, the chiefs and senior petty officers help mold new officers. This critical experience cannot be taught at the Academy or at Officer Training School, and can only be learned from those with the necessary experience. Of course, the Academy's upper classes will have the opportunity to take a summer cruise aboard a cutter to gain some experience before they're commissioned.

Of the approximately 6,000 applicants to the Coast Guard Academy each year, less than

The training ship *Eagle* has all its sails deployed and is at full speed. It was once the German Navy *Horst Wessel*, and the beautiful craft was taken by the U.S. after World War II and became a training ship for the Coast Guard. She has only suffered one major mishap when her bow was crushed during a collision, but repairs were quickly made and she is as good as new. *USCG*

6 percent are admitted to the first year as cadets, and, of that total, almost one-third are women and 20 percent minorities. Candidates must be between the ages of 17 and 22. There are approximately 900 cadets in all four classes at the Academy, which was founded in 1876.

Unlike the other military services, Coast Guard personnel "re-up" on a routine basis. Retention of staff is so great that recruiting is not a high priority, and there are far fewer Coast Guard recruiting offices than any of the other services.

Coast Guard personnel find it difficult to trade their life of protecting people, guarding the environment, and defending the homeland for a small pension or a desk in an office. The work and responsibility ensure a high retention rate, as well as excitement and danger at every turn.

Coast Guard Ensign

While a specific flag for a government agency is rare, the U.S. Coast Guard proudly flies its own colors. The Coast Guard ensign or flag is flown from cutters, patrol craft, and shore stations. A variation of the ensign is flown at U.S. Customs houses and aboard U.S. Customs inspection vessels.

The rationale underlying the use of a separate ensign for the Coast Guard is straightforward—it is a law-enforcement agency first. The ensign is a visible sign of its authority as such. The Coast Guard is a major component of the Department of Homeland Security, yet was previously part of the Department of Transportation and prior to that incarnation, the Treasury Department. All other military organizations are part of the Department of Defense, and although they may have decorative flags, the Coast Guard is the only service with law-enforcement authority. Even when U.S. Navy destroyers and frigates patrol the Eastern Pacific and Caribbean for drug smuggling, they must embark a Coast Guard Law Enforcement Detachment (LEDET) to enforce the law. The LEDET program began in 1982, and was formalized into law in 1986.

The ensign, is never flown at parades and never supplants the national ensign. Secretary of the Treasury Oliver Wolcott created the first design in 1799, and, with minor changes including the addition of the twin Coast Guard anchors, the design has remained unchanged. Secretary Wolcott established the design based on the 13 colonies that signed the Declaration of Independence. His father was one of the signatories of the document, and he created the ensign out of respect for the brave men who fought in the Revolutionary War.

Initially, the ensign was flown when the Revenue Cutters would stop and board suspicious vessels off the coast of the new nation and during examinations and seizures. Soon, the ensign flew at the masthead at all times to signify that the United States had a force at sea that could enforce its maritime and revenue laws. The U.S. Coast Guard has been gradually created and amalgamated from related organizations for over 200 years and has always carried out its diverse missions.

The *Island*-class patrol boat *Monhegan* returns from a drug interdiction on April 26, 2003, with over 2,000 pounds of marijuana and three smugglers. So far, the *Monhegan* has successfully carried out eight anti-drug missions. *USCG*

CHAPTER 1

Organization of the U.S. Coast Guard

A San Diego Coast Guard Air Base rescue swimmer said, "If I have to die to save someone, that's OK." For his willingness to make the ultimate sacrifice, the U.S. Coast Guard pays him $1,800 per month plus minimum housing and medical allowances. He chose the Coast Guard because it is committed to saving lives rather than taking them. However, the Coast Guard is prepared to enforce the law of the sea, which could mean taking lives. At first I attributed the enthusiasm of the rescue swimmer quoted above to his youth, but every Coastie I met shared the same feeling. These men and women—including volunteers (Coast Guard Auxiliary), reservists, and civilians—are willing to sacrifice their own lives when the lives of others are at stake. This is not a recent phenomenon.

A saying from about 1899 would eventually become the Coast Guard byword, "You have to go out, but you do not have to come back." Captain Patrick Etheridge was stationed at the Cape Hatteras Life Saving Station when a vessel smashed into Diamond Shoals and began to break up. People were dying on the quickly sinking ship. As the lifesaving boat was launched and the trained surf men took their places at their oar pulling stations, one of the seamen shouted above the howling wind that they might make it out to the wreck, but not back. The grizzled old skipper reminded them of the admonition in their guidebook that stated they had to go out, but did not say a damn thing about coming back.

The Cape Hatteras Life Saving Station became world famous for its efforts to rescue people in mortal danger in all weather conditions, and, in 1909, the surf men won a gold lifesaving medal and seven silver medals for their rescue of stranded seamen and passengers from the SS *Brewster* in the treacherous Diamond Shoals. This same station won countless medals over the years for saving lives and sometimes paying dearly with their own.

The U.S. military already had a series of government-sanctioned citations and medals for deeds that were above and beyond the call of duty. Personnel that comprised the predecessors of the U.S. Coast Guard also performed courageous acts. The U.S. Congress finally recognized that the Life Saving Service should be allowed to receive medals for daring and heroic acts.

In 1874, Congress created first and second class citations for rescues on the waters of the United States. In 1882, the awards were changed to gold and silver lifesaving medals for demonstrating extreme heroism in the face of impossible odds to save another or others who are in peril in the water.

These awards are not given lightly—they require great sacrifice and courage. Sometimes, the citation is for going out, but not coming back. This creed remained in print until after the Life Saving Service was amalgamated with the U.S. Coast Guard, and continued as the organization began to acquire all of the related services provided by the Federal government. It persisted beyond 1934 when the *Instructions for U.S. Coast Guard Stations* was published, and continues to be an unwritten code for all who belong to America's maritime guardian.

The motto of the U.S. Coast Guard is *Semper Paratus,* which translates into "always ready." It is also the title of the Coast Guard's official anthem and the code under which thousands of men and women have lived and died. It was originally penned by Captain Francis Saltus Van Boskerck in 1922 aboard his cutter, the *Yamacraw,* while it was moored in Savannah, Georgia. It had previously appeared on the ensigns flown by Coast Guard-type vessels as early as 1910.

The Coast Guard has refined its values into three cores elements: Honor or integrity and ethical conduct in all situations; respect for the diversity of all humanity; and simple devotion to duty. They are easy words to say, but very difficult values to sustain in the face of adversity. This is what gives the Coast Guard its rare identity and makes it the American maritime jack of all trades.

The organization also strongly believes in the concept of wherever or whenever the nation or a U.S. citizen needs them. Coast Guard staff will always obey the basic law of the sea to save lives regardless of nationality.

The U.S. Coast Guard serves as a model for many other nations that maintain coast guards of their own. For example, Portugal employs the Guarda-Costa, and many other nations have copied the signature diagonal stripe on the hulls of their cutters to emulate the United States.

U.S. Coast Guard vessels and aircraft are often spared attacks by guerrilla forces and belligerent nations because their white hulls, buff-colored stacks, and masts convey a purpose that is non-threatening. Despite having weapons, which are generally covered with blue tarps, the cutters and patrol craft are peaceful in nature. This makes them welcome, and, in a strange way, gives them a degree of armor or safety. The color schemes have also been immensely popular with the public. Icebreakers are painted red for better identification in the ice, and some classes of helicopters and embarked rigid-hull inflatables are often red in color for easy identification.

This diagonal stripe (slash) of one large orange stripe followed by a blue stripe was created by the design firm of Raymond Loewy/William Snaith, Inc., and was adopted by the entire service on April 6, 1967. The slash was one of the changes made when the Coast Guard was transferred in 1967 to the Department of Transportation from its former 177-year home with the Treasury Department. Aside from the distinctive slash, the Coast Guard emblem is stamped on the orange portion, and the words *Coast Guard* are written on the hull or side of the aircraft. Certain craft (harbor tugs, buoy tenders) are painted black and still have the distinctive slash, but *Raider* port security boats are gray with shadowed lettering that says *U.S. Coast Guard.*

The slash is canted at 64 degrees and has been widely copied by other nations, sometimes in different color schemes (green,

The cutter *Storis* is based out of Kodiak, Alaska. The *Storis* was built in 1944, and has saved countless lives in its career. She will soon be retired. *USCG*

black, orange). The vessels of Sweden's coast guard, or Kbv (Kustbevakning), have royal blue hulls and a pair of angular yellow stripes on the forward hull just aft of the anchors at a 64-degree angle. They, like so many coast guard forces afloat or in the air, are multi-functional. It is interesting that Sweden created a coast guard in 1638, but took until January 7, 1988, to separate it from its customs-collection role.

Their vessels are designed for the rough seas of the Baltic, and, like so many other national coast guards, are designed for the waters adjacent to their national boundaries. The U.S. Coast Guard ventures farther out to sea than any other coast guard, but many nations have adopted the 200-mile exclusion for economic zones and employ larger and armed vessels to protect their resources.

On July 30, 2003, "Coastie," a toy safety boat, is demonstrated by Coast Guard auxiliary personnel in Grand Haven, Michigan, to boaters and their children as part of a boating safety program. The auxiliary performs many duties, including safe-boating education and free boat inspections for safety deficiencies. *USCG*

Older U.S. Coast Guard Patrol Craft and Cutters Never Die

Many nations are using former U.S. Coast Guard patrol boats and cutters, including *Point*-class or smaller 44-foot surf boats. Argentina now utilizes a number of 44-foot surf boats for rescue and inland patrol. In 2002, several ex-Coast Guard vessels found homes with the coast guards or patrol forces of other nations, such as the ex-*Buttonwood* (WLB-306) that ended up in the Dominican Republic; the ex-*Bittersweet* (WLB-389) that was transferred to Estonia; and the ex-*Persistent* (WMEC-6) that will ultimately end up with the Great Lakes Maritime Academy as a training vessel. The *Persistent* was a medium-endurance-class cutter). The ex-*Point Brower* (WPB-82372) served as one of the two remaining 83-foot *Point*-class patrol boats in active service until early 2003, when it was refurbished and sold to Azerbaijan, a former Soviet republic. The ex-*Point Bridge* was transferred to Costa Rica, the ex-*Point Estero* went to Columbia, and the ex-*Point Hannon* went to the Republic of Panama in 2002. The ex-*Point Lobos* has found a new home with the National Oceanographic and Atmospheric Administration, and is a welcome addition to their aging fleet of craft.

The United States left several *Point*-class patrol craft in the hands of the Vietnamese navy/coast guard during the early 1970s, and the craft quickly fell into the hands of the North Vietnamese when they defeated South Vietnam in 1975. Even with minimal maintenance, a few of these durable craft could still be seen knocking around Vietnamese waters as late as the 1990s.

As long as the cutter floats and does its job, it stays in service. This is also the unspoken motto of the *Mackinaw*. To ensure that over 200,000 tons of vital cargo moves efficiently through ice-ridden waters so commerce won't be hindered, the Coast Guard utilizes the well-maintained *Mackinaw*, built in 1944, and newer icebreaking vessels to keep the waterways open for ship traffic. A new *Mackinaw* will replace the almost ancient mariner in 2005. The same is true of the *Storis*, the Queen of the Fleet medium-endurance cutter based out of Kodiak, Alaska. The near-legendary *Storis* will eventually be replaced by a vessel with greater electronic capability and smaller crew requirements.

A Day in the Life of the U.S. Coast Guard

Every day in the U.S. Coast Guard can be different from the last depending on the season and the weather. Winter brings ocean gales, ice, and danger from the frozen north. Summer brings alcohol consumption and high-speed boats on the sea and inland waterways, which becomes a race to save people from themselves. Despite the size of their craft, training, and experience, many of the finest amateur yachtsmen and sailors too often turn their backs on the unforgiving sea. It is then that the men and women of the U.S. Coast Guard must place themselves alongside those in danger to save them. On average, these men and women in blue achieve the following every day:

- Carry out 109 search and rescue missions.
- Save 10 lives from a watery grave.
- Protect nearly $3 million in property.
- Make 396 small-boat sorties for a variety of missions.
- Fly 164 missions in fixed- and rotary-wing aircraft.
- Board and search 144 vessels for contraband, illegal drugs, terrorists, and weapons by Law Enforcement Teams (LEDET).
- Seize nearly $10 million worth of illegal drugs on the high seas and detain smugglers for arraignment and trial.
- Intercept and rescue up to 14 illegal immigrants, who often require medical treatment.
- Inspect 100 vessels for port safety issues by marine specialists.
- Respond to 20 or more oil or pollutant spills in waterways and ports.
- Investigate six vessel wreckages or casualties that involve grounding, sinking, fire, or collision.
- Repair or replace 135 Aids to Navigation (ATON), or buoys, markers, lights, and so forth, to ensure safe passage for vessel traffic. This represents some 20 percent of the Coast Guard's overall workload.
- Assist over 2,500 vessels entering U.S. ports through the Vessel Traffic Service.
- Provide safe passage for vessels during Great Lakes ice season.
- Maintain International Ice Patrol to plot and warn mariners of icebergs in response to the RMS *Titanic* disaster.
- Inspect 377 small craft for safety hazards and conduct 550 classes in boating safety.

Evolution of the U.S. Coast Guard's Organization

The Coast Guard began as a tax and law-enforcement entity that developed in the wake of American independence. It has grown from a small 10-ship Revenue Cutter Service to a multi-faceted organization that has combined other government functions into the present-day U.S. Coast Guard.

The idea of concentrating all maritime-related agencies finally took hold in 1915 when the Life Saving Service and the Revenue Cutter Service were combined to form the designated U.S. Coast Guard. By 1939, the final element, the Lighthouse Service, was brought under the Coast Guard's umbrella. Over 1,000 lighthouses had been constructed in locations throughout the nation and its possessions. Many of these, including the famous lightships, have now been automated and are serviced as aids to navigation. But the romantic lure and lore of these magnificent structures

The cutter *Dauntless* is moored in New Orleans on April 25, 2003, as an MH-68A Stingray makes a run over the harbor area as part of homeland security. *USCG*

will always be a part of U.S. maritime history and signify the first efforts of a new nation to protect seagoing traffic.

The nation's oldest and most prestigious maritime agency, the Coast Guard is a government service unique in its roles, missions, and service. It saves lives, enforces the law, is a potent fifth member of the nation's armed forces, and is a core element of the nation's newest member, the Department of Homeland Security. Since the terrorist attacks in 2001, the nation has looked to some form of inner protection against one of the most dreaded forms of warfare—terrorism. The Department of Homeland Security protects the nation's 95,000 miles of coastline and millions of square miles of exclusive economic zones (to a 200-mile limit from the U.S. shoreline).

Protecting dedicated economic zones is not an exclusively American ideal. Sweden, Denmark, many Baltic nations, and others that rely on the sea for sustenance are reconfiguring their navies to defend their coastal territories. Nations not actively pursuing this course are rethinking the concept of maintaining a blue-water navy that will probably be scrapped in 20 to 30 years without having fired a shot in anger. Many nations such as Norway, Spain, Germany, Singapore, and various South American countries are moving toward a littoral, small-ship development. Sweden has taken a decisive stance in its development of the small-ship navy led by the revolutionary *Visby*-class corvette. The *Visby* class will initially consist of 15 ships constructed of stealth materials (PVC with carbon fiber and vinyl laminate).

Vessels in the small-ship navy are 73 meters long and carry surface-to-air missiles, a rotary wing aircraft, mine-clearing equipment, and other equipment necessary to fight and defeat any foe they might encounter. Aside from being warships, they can also double as coastal patrol and rescue vessels. The underlying principle is that the future of sea warfare and coastal asset management will depend on having the most advanced technology and information systems. Sweden and other forward-thinking nations are leading a revolution in naval/coast guard operations designed to protect their homelands, save lives, and watch over the environment. A small vessel with smart weapons will be best suited to outthink a large and expensive opponent festooned with weapons.

Laws have been established to prevent foreign nations and greedy commercial interests from looting our natural seaborne resources. But even with these laws in place, ocean-going cutters and Coast Guard aircraft continually locate, seize, fine, and impound craft that sneak into the exclusive economic zones with the intent of scooping up thousands of salmon or other endangered fish and any other protected ocean life. Cutters operating in the Bering Sea and near Hawaii routinely bring in thousands of pounds of netting that traps and kills sea turtles and dolphins and poses hazards to navigation. Other nations with economic zones extending 200 miles out to sea face similar problems, but they are challenging them in ways different from the United States. Some have actually bumped ships, rammed one another, and sent warships to drive off interlopers. Some nations have banded together to present an united front to those who violate laws.

When the Integrated Deepwater Project is fully operational, the Coast Guard will be able to face and defeat those who violate our economic zones. The United States will then possess something akin to what Sweden and its neighbors are grasping for—technology and the means to utilize available information to achieve a tactical advantage. Smaller and faster cutters with helicopter support and real-time information will greatly assist the United States in its thrust to defend its economic zones and the natural resources within them.

Formal Organization of the U.S. Coast Guard
The Coast Guard is organized into 14 districts nationwide, with its headquarters in Washington, D.C. and the U.S. Coast Guard Academy in New London, Connecticut. Specialized training schools, a recruiting command, and a vast number of support functions are distributed throughout the United States. Each district is staffed based on demonstrated needs and ever-changing political requirements.

The Coast Guard is the largest of the many organizations within the newly established Department of Homeland Security. Other organizations in the department include the U.S. Customs Service, Immigration and Naturalization Service, Federal Emergency Management Agency (FEMA), Nuclear Incident Response Team (Energy), National BW Defense Analysis Center, and the Secret Service. More than 190,000 employees work in the Department of Homeland Security, and their overall responsibility is to defend the United States from within and reduce the probability that the tragedies of September 11, 2001 are never repeated. The U.S. Coast Guard is perfectly suited for this role, since it has already been charged with defending major elements of the nation's waterways. This role will be significantly expanded as the task of protecting the United States from terrorism and other threats is acknowledged as being one of the largest and most difficult operations in U.S. history. There is no doubt that the Department of Homeland Security and the Coast Guard is up to this challenge.

Ratings and Job Programs in the U.S. Coast Guard

The men and women of the Coast Guard are organized somewhat parallel to the other military services and employ the "E" grade system for pay and ranking. There are 17 major enlisted programs with 3 in the deck and ordnance group, 4 in the engineering and hull group, 3 in the aviation group, and 7 in the administrative and scientific group.

Of great importance, even in this age of high-technology systems, is the boatswain's mate. They are the most versatile and essential members of the Coast Guard's team at sea and in seamanship. Trained in every aspect of driving small craft, boatswain's mates are indispensable aboard any cutter, and ships and small craft do not move safely through the water without them. The ever-present and essential boatswain's mate comprise the oldest seagoing profession in maritime history. They are the masters of seamanship, and when operating a 47-foot search-and-rescue craft that is rolling badly (even over), it is the "boats," as they are often called, that ensure the craft and its crew are safe and that the mission is completed.

Another important enlisted rating is that of electrician's mate. As soon as cutters went to steam power and dynamos were installed for limited electrical power, someone had to operate this new machinery. Electrician's mates became valued members of all crews aboard vessels that are 110 feet or larger.

The aviation maintenance technician (AMT) is responsible for duties such as working aboard the four-engine HC-130 Hercules as a flight engineer, loadmaster, or dropmaster. With additional intense training, the AMT will also become qualified to become an aircrew member aboard a rescue or drug/migrant interdiction rotary-wing aircraft operating from shore stations or cutters. Related to the AMT is the aviation survival technician (AST), whose role is to train pilots and aircrews in survival techniques at sea, including safely exiting a downed aircraft. ASTs are also helicopter rescue swimmers and often have to leap out of hovering helos to save a person who's drowning. The rescue swimmer may also have to accompany a rescue basket to retrieve a number of people from a sinking vessel.

For example, Chief Petty Officer Darren Reeves saved the lives of 26 crew from the foundering cruise liner M/V *Sea Breeze I* on December 17, 2000. As a rescue swimmer, he was lowered from the HH-60 Jayhawk to the wildly plunging deck of the sinking cruise ship. The search-and-rescue helicopter had carried him from the Coast Guard base at Elizabeth City, North Carolina, about 200 miles out to sea in the midst of a hurricane. Reeves was able to save 26 of the crew in his helo, and the remaining 8 were plucked off the deck of the ship just before it went down. Aviation survival technicians can be called upon to do much and many are certified Emergency Medical Technicians (EMTs). In

2003, the beginning salary for this rating was $1,800 per month plus other allowances.

Other enlisted positions are available, including public affairs, storekeeping, information technology, and marine science technician. With the Coast Guard, most of the positions require spray in your face.

Staff Codes and Principles

Another key element in the Coast Guard program is to complete a mission successfully, and not always by the rule book. Occasionally, there is no time to radio for specific instructions, and the leader on the scene, who could be a junior enlisted rating, must make critical decisions. The Coast Guard grants that the principle of on-scene initiative is necessary to allow a degree of personal leadership latitude for the mission to succeed. Coast Guard personnel are able to make decisions without constantly going up and down the chain of command. This is one of the reasons the screening process for selecting both enlisted personnel and officers is so stringent. This service cannot afford indecisive leadership in an emergency. It also cannot afford a trained, robotic response because many disasters and emergencies require individual judgment and on-scene initiative. Managed risk, maximum command flexibility, and obedience to the obvious code of restraint are also stressed in the Coast Guard lexicon.

Having a mission direction and knowing the chain of command are critical to success in any operation, yet the mission can change, and with it, the entire scope of expectations. This roughly translates into the principle of unity of effort, which can mean that additional leaders are inserted into a planned operation.

The Swedish Coast Guard vessel *Kbv-202* carries out a number of missions for the relatively new department. This vessel weighs over 800 tons and oversees fisheries violations and enforces traffic. *Author's Collection*

Alexander Hamilton was wise beyond his years and in his knowledge of the sea. He explained in great detail what was expected of the ten cutter built for and used by the Revenue Marine. In essence, he defined a principle known as effective presence. In other words, a cutter or small craft should not regularly patrol an area so as to allow smugglers to set their clocks by the comings and goings of the Revenue Marine. This would nullify the value of the service and permit thousands of dollars worth of untaxed goods to come and go without being intercepted. The idea was to alter schedules to ensure that smugglers wouldn't know where to land or where a cutter might appear. This principle permitted a 10-vessel force to seemingly multiply itself without adding additional ships.

Saving lives is one thing, but arresting suspected smugglers is another. If the suspects are U.S. citizens, they are entitled to due process and humane restraint. The idea of humane restraint was a strongly worded caution in the U.S. code as written by Treasury Secretary Hamilton in 1791—*U.S. citizens are your countrymen and deserve humane treatment without a domineering spirit.*

Aircraft and Vessels Assigned to Coast Guard Districts

Aircraft and vessel assets are assigned to Coast Guard districts based on the district's historical needs, its demographics, and its type of waterways. For example, illegal-drug forces would not be allocated to the Midwest; barges and small river craft would be assigned for inland water work there. The Coast Guard has always struggled for funds to carry out increasingly demanding missions and has had to borrow aging vessels and aircraft from the U.S. Navy. Old U.S. Navy four-piper flush-deck destroyers that pre-dated World War I were held together by intrepid Coast Guardsmen to chase many rumrunners in the 1920s. Many Coast Guard ratings have to use living quarters from other agencies that have abandoned buildings near their bases of operations. In the early 1950s, one station had to rely upon the graciousness of a gasoline station owner to use his restroom until they could build a shower and other bathroom facilities. Fortunately, this has not really bothered the men and women

of this service. An enlisted men's club or officers' club are rarities only reserved for the few large facilities.

Certain bases are often committed to a number of functions, such as the San Diego Air Station, which has several small rescue craft and search-and-rescue helicopters. The now-closed McClellan Air Force Base Facility, Coast Guard Air Station—Sacramento, hosts four HC-130H Hercules long-range reconnaissance fixed-wing aircraft. These aircraft are 4 of 22 that are in continuous service while the other five are under repair and maintenance.

Coast Guard Island, located in Alameda, California, is the base for the 378-foot high-endurance cutters *Boutwell, Sherman, Morgenthau,* and *Munro* that patrol worldwide. Coast Guard Island also serves as a training and recruit center for the West Coast. The *Boutwell* was one of the major Coast Guard ships committed to Operation Iraqi Freedom, and its crew performed magnificently. Two squadrons of four 110-foot *Island*-class patrol craft were also deployed, and another high-endurance cutter was deployed in the Mediterranean. Port Security Units (PSU) were assigned, and an ocean-going *Juniper*-class buoy tender—the USCG *Walnut* (WLB-205)—journeyed all the way from Hawaii. The primary focus was to emancipate the Iraqi people from the despotic regime of Saddam Hussein and provide humanitarian relief. Over 1,200 Coast Guard personnel were involved, while the other 97 percent of the Coast Guard's personnel continued with their duties at home.

Certain stations such as Noyo Harbor in northern California and Bodega Bay have smaller search-and-rescue craft such as the new

47-foot all-aluminum boats and the 87-foot *Marine Protector*-class patrol boats that can go out in almost any sea state to rescue boaters and others caught in trouble at sea. Although the 47-foot aluminum SAR craft is an excellent platform for rescuing people at sea, it does not do well retrieving people stranded on rocky pinnacles among the waves. The smaller rigid-hull inflatable boats are best suited for this task.

San Francisco, California; Newport, Rhode Island; Honolulu, Hawaii; and many other stations are ports for seagoing buoy tenders that replace and repair buoys and other aids to navigation. Buoy tenders patrol inland rivers and waterways as well.

Aside from the 35,000 Coast Guard staff, there are 8,000 reservists that can be called upon to serve at any time. They routinely train with their full-time counterparts and keep abreast of new policies, procedures, and equipment. This force may swell to 10,000 staff in the near future to give the Coast Guard a surge capability to meet various crises around the nation and abroad. Over 4,300 of the reserve staff was mobilized during Operation Iraqi Freedom.

This force is further augmented with an Auxiliary of 35,000 men and women who assist and fill in whenever necessary.

The Auxiliary, which donates over two million hours of time to the Coast Guard each year, was created in 1939 by Congress to assist Coast Guard staff in non-law-enforcement roles. Auxiliary members receive training that keeps them up-to-date on Coast Guard protocol. Since 1996, the Coast Guard Authorization Act has allowed the Auxiliary greater latitude in what it can do to assist the service. This has been greatly helpful to the Coast Guard.

Auxiliary membership is limited to those who are at least 17-years-old, a citizen of the United States, and a former member of any branch of the United States military. Since the Auxiliary was added to the overall force structure of the Coast Guard, it has logged thousands of hours of vital support in five mission areas crucial to the success of the overall operations of the Coast Guard.

The Auxiliary offers public education courses in small-boat handling and safety, understanding navigation aids, and recognizing hazards and danger.

The Auxiliary will inspect a private craft for free to let the owner know what is missing or if the boat needs attention to increase safety on the water. If the boat passes the examination, it is given a Vessel Safety Check (VSC) sticker that shows Coast Guard personnel that the boat complies with basic safe-boating requirements. If the boat fails the examination, the Auxiliary officer provides a list of deficiencies. The Auxiliary has saved countless lives by preventing accidents through this program.

These men and women also teach the basic rules of the water. More than ever piloting small craft in increasingly crowded harbors are under the watchful eye of Homeland Security Patrols. The Auxiliary also assist the regular and reserve Coast Guard in a variety of missions including marine safety, patrolling marine and pleasure events on the water, and certifying that personal flotation devices and EPIRBS (Emergency Position-Indicating Radio Beacons) for those who are lost at sea are in working order.

This is the Noyo Harbor Coast Guard Station in Fort Bragg, California. Here two 47-foot surf boats and a rigid-hull inflatable are assigned to various missions, including protecting valuable salmon fishing areas from poachers and search-and-rescue operations. *Author's Collection by Hunter Lanzaro*

The Coast Guard Auxiliary wears a variation of the Coast Guard uniform and has its own ranking system. Members make periodic pleasure vessel inspections and introduce high-school juniors to the possibility of an education at the Coast Guard Academy. Under Project AIM (Academy Introduction Mission),

220 students are given the opportunity to stay at the Coast Guard Academy for a week during the summer to find out what it takes to become a Coast Guard officer.

Added to the regular Coast Guard, its reserve force, and auxiliary, are approximately 5,500 civilian employees. Considering the total, the force structure is still much smaller than any of the other military services.

Patrol Craft, Cutters, and Aircraft

Since its inception, the Coast Guard has been underfunded and frequently has had to seek vessels and equipment from other services or the mothball and reserve fleets. The famous medium-endurance cutter *Tamoroa*, which was featured in the book and film *The Perfect Storm* was once a U.S. Navy salvage tug that was borrowed after World War II. It was eventually repainted Coast Guard white with the signature slash on the hull. The craft was decades old when the Coast Guard used it in the storms of the North Atlantic. Recently, there has been an effort to rebuild the aging fleet of patrol craft, cutters, and aircraft. The Coast Guard has introduced the 47-foot surf/rescue craft, which can roll completely over and still right itself. The service has also begun to replace its fleet of icebreakers and buoy tenders as well as its helicopters and patrol boats. The 87-foot *Marine Protector* class has been assigned to the smaller coastal stations in tandem with SAFE (Secure All-around Flotation Equipped) boats, which are 23-foot-long rigid-hull inflatable craft. The 110-foot *Island* class will ultimately undergo a vast improvement in its overall capabilities, including a 13-foot extension on the stern to launch rigid-hull inflatables. All of these craft are being rebuilt to withstand higher sea states and endure and survive in heavier weather. The 110-foot patrol boat *Matagorda*, based in Miami, Florida, has already been turned over to the Bollinger Shipyard in Louisiana for the first of many 110-foot *Island*-class conversions.

Fighting the tide of illegal drugs is a significant challenge for the U.S. Coast Guard and a major function of its cutters, helicopters, and fixed-wing aircraft in the Caribbean and eastern Pacific. The seizure rate of drugs is phenomenal, but has required warships from the U.S. Navy to help stem the flow. The best that the Coast Guard has ever projected for their part in this effort is a reduction of illegal drugs by over 18 percent per year. Drug runners are far more sophisticated than the rumrunners of the 1920s prohibition era. Drug cartels have surveillance teams in all ports bordering the Caribbean and eastern Pacific and know when a patrol boat is in the vicinity. In response, the Coast Guard and Navy are using armed helicopters (MH-90 Enforcers) and U.S. Navy Seahawks that can disable a boat's engine. This is an example of the respect for human rights that is afforded to suspected drug runners. U.S. anti-drug forces on the high seas avoid killing suspects and have developed weapons that will stop a drug-running "go-fast" craft traveling at 50 knots.

The Coast Guard has been very successful at interdicting illegal drugs and has kept over $10 billion (street value) worth of cocaine and marijuana off U.S. streets over the last 10 years. Nearly 500 vessels have been seized and scores of go-fast craft have been sunk or disabled. The danger to Coast Guard law-enforcement personnel (LEDET) is growing despite training in weapons and strategies for boarding suspicious vessels offered at the Petaluma, California, training center. The use of helicopters and unmanned aircraft to survey a vessel before a boarding team arrives helps protect personnel who might encounter anything from a knife-wielding thug to a shoulder-held surface-to-surface missile.

Another issue that confronts the Coast Guard daily in the Pacific, Caribbean, and Atlantic is stemming the flow of illegal aliens attempting to enter the United States on virtually anything that will float. Medium-endurance cutters, such as the *Famous* and *Reliance* classes and the 110-foot *Island*-class patrol boats, generally carry out this task. The *Famous* and *Reliance* classes have flight decks for helicopter operations (HH-65 Dolphin, HH-60J Jayhawk), and the vessels frequently return to the United States packed with migrants plucked from rotting watercraft. The owners of these craft often charge the migrants outrageous amounts of money or jewels for passage, and it is unknown how many illegal aliens have perished at sea. Amazingly, the Coast Guard has rescued 149,969 illegal migrants in the last decade. Occasionally, the leaking craft had rudimentary navigation equipment, but little food and water. Many of the craft were tire inner tubes lashed together with planks tied on top. The many occupants suffered exposure to the elements for days as they drifted.

The stories of escaping Cubans, Haitians, Chinese, and others would fill volumes. The United States is not the only country to face this problem. Currently, hundreds of men, women, and children try to make it across the Strait of Gibraltar to Spain from Morocco for a better life. Thousands have died in that nine-mile stretch of water. Once in Europe, the escapees from North Africa blend into the populace. The Spanish, Italian, and Portuguese coast guards attempt to stop the traffic of illegal migrants and have the same difficulties experienced by the United States.

Ultimately, the entire spectrum of Coast Guard aircraft and vessels will come under the auspices of the Integrated Deepwater Program, which is designed to make the Coast Guard a fully modern maritime force for the twenty-first century. This concept is directly related to homeland security and the idea of the National Fleet. The National Fleet model is base on an interrelationship between the Coast Guard and the U.S. Navy. The notion of two separate federal deepwater services with different craft is out of date. The U.S. Navy and Coast Guard will utilize increasingly similar ships so they can operate in tandem and carry out missions more effectively and economically. The U.S. Navy is particularly interested in the Coast Guard's shallow-draft inshore fleet of vessels. The day of the blue-water war fought between opposing navies on a grand scale has passed into history, and future maritime wars will be fought in the littoral or near the shoreline.

Some of the new aircraft and vessels being contemplated for the Coast Guard under the Integrated Deepwater Project are: new maritime patrol aircraft (long-range), unmanned air vehicles (UAVs) for surveillance/long-range observation, improved SAR helicopters, national-security cutters with greater reliance on electronics and fewer human resources, fast-response cutters, and short- and long-range rigid-hull inflatable craft.

The new fleet of air and surface assets will be phased in to replace the aging systems, and a greater number of aircraft and vessels will be available. This is due to the Coast Guard's interoperability with the U.S. Navy and the Department of Homeland Security mandate to protect America's shorelines from terrorists.

The Integrated Deepwater Project will make the Coast Guard the most modern and responsive maritime force in the world today. However, the new assets will not replace or supplant the courage and fortitude of the Coast Guard men and women who will still be on duty at sea, in the air, or at a shore base. The young ensign leading a boarding crew up the slab side of a filthy coastwise freighter suspected of carrying contraband may have the assistance of a device that can give a real-time picture of what is on that hidden deck above. An unmanned aerial vehicle with a camera can do this, but the boarding team will still have to climb the slimy Jacob's ladder to begin their inspection. Technology will help immensely, but critical and practical knowledge of ships and the sea ultimately rest with the men and women of the Coast Guard.

Homeland Security and the Future of the USCG
The terrorist attacks on September 11, 2001, forever changed the way we view our nation and our safety. The United States is no longer safe from this new type of warfare, which is war against civilians rather than the military. This is the way of terrorism—war in the shadows. In order to prevent a reoccurrence, the federal government created a plan to combat this oldest version of fear mongering. Part of this plan is the Department of Homeland Security.

There are 95,000 miles of coastline and scores of ports, coves, and other areas where terrorists could enter the country. Interruption of import and export processes could paralyze the nation, and naval and other military facilities located near the water could be damaged. The task to allow an uninterrupted flow of goods and services to maintain a robust economy and protect the nation from a maritime disaster falls to the U.S. Coast Guard.

On February 25, 2003, Secretary of Transportation Norman Y. Mineta formally transferred the Coast Guard to the Department of Homeland Security. Secretary Tom Ridge assumed control on January 24, 2003 during a formal ceremony in Washington, D.C., with Commandant Collins in attendance. The charge to the Coast Guard is to guard our shore as never before, with the prime threat now being terrorism. This will require more equipment and other assets and experienced top-notch personnel who can anticipate a potential enemy's every move. The Coast Guard realizes the gravity of the task and is always ready.

The old lighthouse at Havre de Grace on the Chesapeake Bay once attempted to repulse British forces who tried to fight their way to the nation's capital during the War of 1812. Now its rusty cannon stands as mute evidence of the bravery of a family who loved their new land so much they would fight a superior force with a tiny weapon. *Author's Collection*

History of the U.S. Coast Guard

The Treasury Department Establishes the U.S. Lighthouse Service

Providing aids to navigation (ATON) is one of the important responsibilities of the federal government. In 1789, there was no Coast Guard and very little federal government. But Alexander Hamilton, the first Secretary of the Treasury, realized the need for safe passageways for vessels entering and departing U.S. waters. If merchant ships and commerce coming and going from U.S. ports were not guaranteed safety from natural disaster (shoals, wrecks, rocks, shallows, and such), trade would be severely hampered and the new country's reputation would be tarnished.

The nation had just emerged from a war of revolution, and, next to civil wars, these are the most costly. The new country was on the verge of bankruptcy during its first few months of existence. The central government worked with local municipalities and states to provide rudimentary services, but a source of stable income was necessary to pay prior debts and provide a financial base to build a future and a dependable revenue stream. Income tax was unheard of at the time, so customs and tonnage taxes on vessels became an important source of revenue.

When the Revolutionary War ended, there were 12 lighthouses along U.S. waterways, most of which were erected by local interests.

The Boston Lighthouse, located near the entrance to Boston Harbor, has been in operation since 1716 and is generally considered the oldest continuously operating lighthouse in the United States. It is still operational and has been modified with a more powerful lens system. It is also different from most American lighthouses because it is fully manned by three Coast Guard lightkeepers. It has a rich history and witnessed the battle between the American warship *Chesapeake* and the British frigate HMS *Shannon*. During this particular battle, the *Chesapeake*'s commanding officer, Captain James Lawrence, reportedly told his crew, "Don't give up the ship." The lighthouse was destroyed by the British during the Revolutionary War and was rebuilt in 1783. Its seven-foot-thick walls made of brick and mortar made it quite difficult to level, but easy to rebuild.

The 280-year-old structure has been guiding ships in and out of Boston Harbor safely with lenses (invented by French Physicist Augustin Fresnel in 1822) that could take a single candlepower and magnify it so it could be seen 12 miles away.

Dozens of other stone lighthouses were built by the colonies, and small smooth-bore cannons guarded many. One such structure was located near Havre de Grace, Maryland. A cannon at the water's edge was reputed to have been repeatedly fired by the lighthouse keeper and his family as British craft attempted to sail up to Washington, D.C. during the War of 1812. The small cannon was barely big enough to fit into the back of a pickup truck, but it caused a great nuisance to the raiding British who repeatedly tried to silence it. The lighthouse is still standing, and the rusted cannon still maintains its lonely vigil.

All lighthouses and stations came under the control of the Department of the Treasury on August 7, 1789, which makes it the oldest forerunner of today's Coast Guard. In a sense, the Coast Guard began with aids to navigation (ATON). The federal government nationalized all aids to navigation that were previously built, serviced, and maintained by private parties, colonies, cities, and municipalities. Many were little more than bluffs where fires could be built during storms to warn ships of rocks and shoals, and others were relatively well-built brick structures with lamps that could be seen for miles.

Ultimately, over 1,000 lighthouses were built in the United States, its trust territories, and possessions. The first steam-powered lightship tender, the USRC *Shubrick,* was built prior to the Civil War. Its 12-knot speed on a 140-foot-long hull was perfect for the many other duties assigned to vessels that served the Revenue Cutter Service. In addition to the lighthouses, lightships helped guide the incoming ships to safety.

Eventually, entire classes of lighthouse tenders were built as the Lighthouse Service was bounced from agency to agency in the federal government. But no one disputed the value of this aid to navigation and the thousands of people who helped ensure that mariners were kept safe in U.S. waters. Finally, the Lighthouse Service ended up in the Revenue Marine Bureau, a division of the Department of the Treasury in 1845, where it remained relatively untouched and adequately funded. Fog bells were added as well as trumpets and an air siren in 1887. Each organizational change seemed to bring about more improvements in the Lighthouse Service.

The final organizational change happened on July 1, 1939, when the Lighthouse Service was combined with the U.S. Coast Guard. With the service came all of the navigational systems and a substantial part of the Coast Guard's work. Although the basic buoy is not as romantic as the statuesque old lighthouse, it has saved many lives. The Lighthouse Service experienced more changes in the field of personnel reduction through automation. This in turn led to additional lights being added in difficult locales where the weather and terrain almost forbade human habitation. An example of this is the St. George Reef lighthouse, six miles off the coast of the Oregon/California border.

The SS *Brother Jonathan,* a 220-foot, 1,359-ton paddlewheel steamer, sank in a storm near the St. George reef near Crescent City, California. A lighthouse was built nearly two decades later to warn mariners of the rocks and pinnacles that ripped the bottom out of the *Brother Jonathan.* The structure then became the most expensive lighthouse in U.S. history at $704,633. The lighthouse is now abandoned and in its place, a lighted buoy warns mariners of the area's substantial dangers. A privately funded expedition has located the wreck of the *Brother Jonathan* about 6 miles off the coast and 250 feet under the surface. The vessel,

Two aids to navigation (ATON) have generally fallen into disuse, but are witnesses to history. The lightship *Columbia* once stood guard over the entrance to the Columbia River and its treacherous bar, as did the huge unmanned, lighted buoy. Battery-operated electronic ATONS will eventually replace these items of Americana. *Author's Collection*

once owned by the Vanderbilt interests, was lost with 166 of its crew and passengers on July 30, 1865. Only 19 survived to tell about the harrowing wreck and the desperate struggle to stay alive. They also spread rumors of over $200,000 in Yankee gold pieces, which in their uncirculated condition are worth millions of dollars today. Court battles rage between the discoverers and the State of California over the value of the gold cargo.

The lighthouse atop St. George's Reef off Crescent City, California, is captured on a calm day. It took nearly $1 million and almost 20 years to build, due to the site and the weather. A battery-operated ATON buoy has replaced this ghostly icon on the Pacific coast. *Author's Collection*

The U.S. Revenue Marine (Cutter) Service

The U.S. Congress passed a series of laws in 1789 and 1790 to provide money for the treasury, aids to navigation, and a force to save lives at sea.

The U.S. Revenue Marine Service became the small but innovative enforcer of the nation's laws of the sea. The Revenue Marine Service, which became the Revenue Cutter Service in the 1890s when it acquired purpose-built vessels, enforced the basic laws of the sea around the nation's shores and its inland waterways.

One of the first tasks of the service was to federalize existing lighthouses, no matter what shape they were in. Many were simply piles of stones with crude lighting fixtures maintained to warn mariners of hazards. Aids to navigation became an important, if not very glamorous, responsibility of the new entity, and this soon expanded to buoys and other markers. Taxes and fees that allowed the government to function came from trade sources, and properly marked harbors were crucial to trade. The United States has always been a maritime nation, and protection of trade from hazards such as pirates, tax evaders, and more obvious dangers such as rocks and shoals was foremost in the mind of Alexander Hamilton and those who managed the meager resources of the new nation. Like the Coast Guard of today, there were missions that didn't fit any other agency, so when poachers began stealing lumber and cutting down trees along the coasts, the Revenue Cutter Service was assigned the task of stopping this illegal activity. Armed with the Timber Act of 1822, the Revenue Cutter Service sought out those who stole natural resources from the nation. This laid the foundation for the Coast Guard to enforce the laws that protect our natural resources at sea.

The next task was to ensure that tariffs were paid by traders entering and leaving the United States. The average American seafarer and shipping company realized the need to support the new government, but also grumbled about the taxes and tariffs. The tax and tariff laws was written before the Navy or any other branch of the military service was created. For a decade in the early history of the nation, 10 Revenue Marine Service cutters served as the country's naval power. Those 10 cutters helped the United States see an increase in trade from $52 million per year to $205 million per year.

The 10 cutters were built based on an act passed by Congress and signed into law by President George Washington on August 4, 1790. The government was allowed 10 boats and craft to protect the nation's revenue. Secretary of the Treasury Alexander Hamilton initially sought commissioned naval officers to act as the four officers per cutter, but Congress saw otherwise. There was no Navy at the time, so the Revenue Marine officers that commanded the vessels would have customs officers onboard. This was appropriate since customs officers had arrest powers that naval officers did not have. The Revenue Marine Service was placed under the Treasury Department as its arm at sea to enforce customs and tariff laws and other duties as required. Early cutters had four officers: a master and three mates. An additional four mariners or enlisted personnel and two boys served on each ship.

Hamilton and the early government were so intent on controlling costs that seven of the cutters were built for less than $1,000 each, yet the other three were slightly more expensive because they patrolled in the upper New England states and required stronger construction.

The first commission of a Revenue Marine cutter officer or "Master of a Cutter in the Service of the United States for the Protection of Revenue" was Hopley Yeaton of New

The Revenue cutter *Massachusetts* was built as one of the first 10 Revenue cutters under Alexander Hamilton's program. Unfortunately, the craft was too expensive and was sold a year after it was introduced to the Revenue Marine. It was not built to specification and was too slow despite the fact that it mounted six heavy-duty swivel guns and was crewed by a competent staff. *USCG*

Hampshire. He was awarded his commission on March 21, 1791, and aside from serving as the first quasi-commandant of the Coast Guard, Ship's Master Yeaton was also the first commissioned customs officer to command a Revenue Marine vessel. His ship was the cutter *Scammel,* which was launched on August 24, 1791, at Portsmouth, New Hampshire.

The Revenue Marine cutters were not heavily armed, but they were a solid match for pirates that hung around the southern states waiting for easy prey. Through 1822, cutters with help from the new U.S. Navy and the British Royal Navy finally swept pirates from the Caribbean.

The Revenue Cutter Service laid the groundwork for the U.S. Coast Guard to become the

Steamboats routinely blew up at sea and on inland waters. Finally, the federal government introduced laws to help stem the tide of destruction due to faulty construction, maintenance, and incompetent and untrained engineers. Ships still caught fire, and thousands died, such as on the *General Slocum* on the Hudson River in New York, when 957 out of 1,358 passengers and crew perished within yards of land. Those that escaped fire generally drowned. *Author's Collection*

nation's law-enforcement agent at sea, and today, its shield of freedom. Eventually, other organizations, such as the Lighthouse Service in 1845, would be attached to the Revenue Cutter Service. In 1915, the U.S. Coast Guard emerged, and more organizations would later be added (Bureau of Navigation and Steamboat Inspection in 1946) to create today's Coast Guard to protect the nation and its citizens at sea.

The U.S. Steamboat Inspection Service

The function of steamboat inspection was originally placed under the control of the Justice Department on July 7, 1838. It was transferred to the Treasury Department on August 30, 1852.

Robert Fulton's steamboat, the SS *Clermont* successfully steamed to Albany, New York, in the remarkable time of 32 hours at 4.7 miles per hour in 1807. It may not have been the earliest steamboat, but it was the first one that was 150 feet long and could carry passengers and cargo. With commercial possibilities that boggled the mind, by late 1807 the *Clermont* and its successors became the talk of the rivers for transporting cargo and people. By then, everyone who understood even a modicum of steam propulsion teamed up with shipwrights to built vessels with "teakettles" connected to paddle wheels connected to shafts sticking out of the hull amidships that slapped the water forward or backward. This soon became a problem because the original *Clermont* was actually unfit to carry passengers. Aside from a relatively untried propulsion plant, it was 150 feet in length, had a 13-foot beam, and a freeboard of 4 feet. A length-to-beam ratio of 11.5 feet to 1 foot is appropriate for high-speed experimental craft, but not for untested high-center-of-gravity commercial craft like the *Clermont*, which would never have passed modern standards of safety.

The future was not so rosy for other operators. By 1838, there was a loss rate of 14 percent for steamboats and steamships due to hull problems or boiler explosions. Congress became quite alarmed by the losses and the pressure being exerted by cargo shippers and insurance companies. The losses were staggering and had to be stopped. There was some difference of opinion as to what entity should carry out steamboat inspection and regulation enforcement. "State's righters" believed in strong state governments and a smaller federal government. But ships moving from state-to-state required uniform laws, so the idea of state self-determination was eclipsed by the need for a strong federal government. The explosion of the steamboat SS *Pulaski* off the North Carolina shore in 1837 led to federal laws that helped create the Steamboat Inspection Service.

Laws were passed that required steamboats to be inspected every six months. The inspection included a hull and boiler survey to determine their ability to safely continue service. Unfortunately, the laws did not go far enough and weren't structured to ensure enforcement.

In 1852, Congress again addressed the issue of continued carnage at sea and on inland waterways due to faulty boilers, steam engines, and poorly built hulls. This time, inspectors were appointed to ensure that follow-up was carried out, penalties were assessed against shipping companies, and that pilots and lieutenants were licensed. A civil insurrection intervened in 1861, and many of the advances were reversed due the needs of both the North and the South to prosecute their military causes.

As the nation's dependence on steam power increased after the Civil War, significant efforts were undertaken to make steamships safer. All previous laws and statutes were repealed, and the government carefully examined what was needed to make steam travel safe and secure. New laws and better methods of inspection reduced the number of vessel explosions from faulty steam power plants, but the high incidence of fires onboard ships would again change the role of the Steamboat Inspection Service and completely revamp its organizational structure and placement within the federal government.

U.S. Lifesaving Service

The concept of a lifesaving service can be traced back to China and the Chinkiang Association for the Saving of Life, which was first established in 1708 with organized lifesaving stations, boats, and equipment along the treacherous Yangtze River. The goal was to protect and save the passengers and trained seamen who sailed the coastal routes and inland rivers of China. The boats and junks were specially painted and had sails that identified them as lifesaving vessels. Pirates and barbarous men who were employed by local warlords respected the lifesaving service as being something good and untouchable. A drowning pirate might need the services of the lifesavers association, so to kill the hand that might save you was foolish. This concept of organized lifesaving along coastal routes and inland rivers slowly spread as the West came in contact with China. Soon, lifesaving stations appeared in the

United Kingdom and along the coast of North and Central Americas. Trained seamen were invaluable to ship owners, and methods to preserve their lives were continuously sought.

The Massachusetts Humane Society led the way to save lives at sea from the shoreline, and later from evolutionary and rudimentary surf boats. Founded in 1786, the Massachusetts Humane Society, in conjunction with other related organizations, did what it could with limited resources to save lives and lobby local government for funds to establish a formal organization. Even before the U.S. government allowed any funds for lifesaving, the Massachusetts association set up 18 stations along its coast where the greatest loss of life and property seemed to occur. In 1847, after substantial prodding and much lobbying, the federal government allowed a sum of $4,000 to equip its lighthouses with lifesaving gear such as surf-type boats, rope, and rockets. This was far from enough to solve the problem at hand, and what would come with a growing maritime nation. New Jersey Congressman William A. Newell, who was also a physician, initiated a bill that would fund up to $10,000 for lifesaving stations along the New Jersey coastline. New York soon followed suit in 1849 with a $20,000 appropriation, but despite the major successes in obtaining funding and public support—and the many lives that were saved along the eastern seaboard—there was a huge hole in the system. There were no lifesavers specifically appointed to respond to emergencies and staff the stations to guard the expensive equipment. This notwithstanding, over 2,900 stranded or dying people were saved by intrepid lifesavers with available equipment, and this number edged upward each time a ship grounded during a storm. The concept of a lifesaving service had fully taken hold in 1838.

By 1856, paid lighthouse keepers supervised lifesaving efforts in their regions. Small, garage-like wooden houses dotted the New England coastline. The first originated in Massachusetts and was unattended for the most part. They were called Society Houses of Refuge and were paid for by individual subscribers with little or no government assistance. They served as storage huts for boats, oars, ropes, carts, rockets and such. They also helped the mariner who washed ashore and needed a place to shelter himself from the elements, build afire in the small stove, and have some food before traveling toward a settlement.

By the dawn of the Civil War, there were continued attempts to improve the lifesaving service and acquire better equipment and paid station keepers. Even the overworked revenue cutters were pressed into service as everything was done to save people stranded at sea. The calls upon the limited number of craft and other strained government resources prevented all but a token response to the need. Private citizens continued to help, and groups who lived and earned their incomes from the sea came up with more progressive ideas than the government. The Civil War intervened, and most attempts at establishing a formal lifesaving service slowed considerably. It was not until four years after the unification of the nation that Congress revisited the issue of a formal lifesaving service. It began with an appropriation of $200,000 in 1871 to follow up its promise to have a permanent federal lifesaving keeper at each station.

The year 1872 could be considered a watershed for organized lifesaving along the coastlines of the reunified United States. Sumner I. Kimball, one of the nation's most competent and committed maritime administrators, assumed control of the Revenue Marine and took an active role in the lifesaving aspect of what would become the Coast Guard. When Congress finally established a formal lifesaving service within the Treasury Department in 1878, Kimball was the choice for its superintendent. Within months, there were 189 lifesaving stations nationwide. Of this total, 139 were located on the Eastern seaboard, with 37 around the Great Lakes, 7 on the Pacific Coast, 5 on the Gulf Coast, and 1 located at the Falls of the Ohio River. Finally, by 1878, the world's premier maritime nation had a lifesaving service that really could save lives.

The U.S. Life Saving Service had a formal lifetime of 37 years, from 1878 to 1915, when it was merged with the Revenue Cutter Service to form the U.S. Coast Guard. Kimball served as head of the service until 1915 and continued to serve the cause for many more years, providing guidance on the development and purchase of new lifesaving equipment. After 59 years of public service, Kimball passed away in 1923.

The Formation of the Coast Guard

Actually, the impetus for the formation of the Coast Guard originated with Senator Charles E. Townsend, who introduced it in Senate Bill 2337 on May 26, 1913. The two-page bill provided for the combination of the Life Saving Service and the Revenue Cutter Service and the establishment of the U.S. Coast Guard to perform these duties. The bill also said the Coast Guard would

Even years after many laws have been passed, ships still catch fire. The SS *Morro Castle* burns and soon will drift ashore at Asbury Park, New Jersey. A ship pleasantly touted as a "Havana ferryboat," which was in reality a booze cruiser where young people simply stayed drunk for days; and no command and control caused the situation to get out of hand. The ship was a floating fire trap as it was, and its firefighting equipment was ineffective and of little value. The ship was doomed when the first flames licked at the flammable curtains in the early hours of September 8, 1934. There were 135 deaths, and the laws became even more stringent after this tragedy. The steamboat inspection function was also moved to the newly formed U.S. Coast Guard. *Author's Collection*

fall under the jurisdiction of the U.S. Navy during wartime, but during peacetime, would report to the Secretary of the Treasury.

The bill grandfathered all existing personnel into their current jobs, but allowed for the two division chiefs to have the then-unheard-of salary of $3,000 per year. It also corrected certain inequities that had existed for men and women who had served in the lifesaving service and the Revenue Cutter Service. They were to receive the same benefits as those in the military service. The act was passed through various committees and was ultimately passed by both Houses on March 12, 1914. President Wilson signed the act on January 28, 1915 and the nation had a viable coast guard, but the new organization needed a name. Captain Commandant Ellsworth P. Bertholf and Secretary of the Treasury Hugh McCulloch observed that the Spanish government had a coastal watching service that dated back several hundred years that was known as (and still is) the Guardia Costa. The Guardia Costa was responsible for preventing vessels from engaging in illegal trade. In England, a similar organization had men stationed on the beach to make certain that ships did not unload their cargoes at deserted locations to avoid taxes. In addition, the Spanish Guardia Costa and English Coastguard helped save mariners in distress and acted as naval reservists in time of war. Combined, the duties seemed to define what the United States was seeking from its newest federal entity, and the name was perfect—the Coast Guard.

There was little time to form the new organization before World War I intervened, and by 1917, the Coast Guard was knee deep in military operations. Before the actual transfer from the Treasury Department to the Navy Department, the Coast Guard patrolled harbors, provided port security, and watched over the launch of new U.S. Navy warships against saboteurs. Finally, the order came through on April 6, 1917 to transfer the Coast Guard to the Navy Department, and its role expanded rapidly.

The large ocean-going cutters *Algonquin, Ossipee, Manning, Seneca, Tampa,* and *Yamacraw* were fitted out for distant service off the coast of Europe. Yachts were pressed into service for antisubmarine work, which, in 1917, was all but a joke. It consisted of finding a submarine and radioing a larger heavily armed warship to come and destroy the sub.

A rift between the Navy and the Coast Guard developed when reserve naval officers were given priority rank and billets, while experienced seaman and officers in the Coast Guard were relegated to small patrol craft and the antisubmarine warfare (ASW) yacht patrol. The ocean belonged to the Navy until peacetime.

The ethnicity of many Coast Guard sailors also became an issue. Most of the sailors were of Austro-German descent. With questions of loyalty to the United States, one-year enlistments were changed to three-year terms for the duration of the war. This issue was settled rather quickly and somewhat quietly, however, with the loss of the cutter *Tampa* just weeks before the end of the war. The cutter was sunk by a single torpedo fired from the German *UB-91* in the Bristol Channel, and 111 Coast Guard and four Navy personnel were lost.

The "war to end all wars" came to end on November 11, 1918 and the Coast Guard was

The *Dobbins Lifeboat* was used to rescue people at sea. Its surf crew is aboard, and the wagon will tow the self-bailing boat to the water's edge by horse. Well-wishers help push the craft into the surf. *USCG*

a better organization for the experience. In two years, it gained decades of military experience and organizational structure. From the Navy's viewpoint, the Coast Guard was not the "hooligan navy" it was once touted to be. It was a professional seagoing force that the Navy needed in time of war, and it was clear that the maritime forces needed one another.

The Bureau of Marine Inspection
In 1932, the Steamboat Inspection Service and the Bureau of Navigation were combined into one organization—the Bureau of Marine Inspection. This was the precursor to the Coast Guard's vessel inspection program to assess safety and compliance with U.S. Port Facilities laws and determine how safe a ship was for its crew and passengers.

The early nineteenth century saw a huge increase in the number of steamboats cruising rivers, lakes, and coastal waters around the United States. Unfortunately, many of the new steamboats were slipshod and barely safe enough to pass builder's trials. Steamboats

On April 16, 2003, a Stingray (MH-68A) helicopter is on homeland security patrol over New York City. This aircraft is heavily armed and can respond to virtually any threat posed by those who would harm the U.S. or its citizens. At sea, under Liberty Shield, ships are inspected for contraband and suspected terrorists. The Coast Guard is being as less intrusive as humanly possible to ensure that the rights of all U.S. citizens are maintained at all costs. *USCG*

began to explode, and boilers that should have never been installed failed. People not only had the fear of drowning to contend with, but now, fire was usually accompanied by scalding steam. The only place to turn for redress was the government, which finally responded to the thousands of complaints in 1838. Fourteen percent of all steamboats and steamships that were built from 1832 to 1838 were destroyed by faulty steam engine plants.

Other disasters consumed ships from the Bering Sea to the Caribbean and even up the Mississippi River. Marine inspection for shipboard safety became a paramount issue, and the U.S. government responded with the creation of the Bureau of Marine Inspection. New laws were passed to regulate ship safety and the professional competence of those who operated vessels at sea. In 1942, during World War II, the entire Marine Inspection Service was transferred to the U.S. Coast Guard. The formalities of the transfer happened after the war in 1946.

World War II Operations and the Bureau of Marine Inspection
After the end of World War II, the Coast Guard was released from the control of the Navy Department and transferred back to the Department of the Treasury. The Marine Inspection Service was added, becoming the foundation for a number of changes that would come. Commercial fishing and inland navigation laws fell under the Coast Guard responsibility. Oil pollution prevention methodology and, in cooperation with other nations, the Safety of Life at Sea (SOLAS), have also been added. These services ensure that all foreign passenger, cargo, and tank vessels entering or leaving U.S. ports are inspected by the Coast Guard.

The Department of Transportation Assumes Command of the Coast Guard
The U.S. Coast Guard existed under the Treasury

Department from 1915 until 1967, except during war, when it was under the control of the Navy Department. Changes in the responsibilities of the Coast Guard became evident in 1967. The Vietnam War was winding down for the Coast Guard, and the 200-mile economic resources zones and 12-mile fisheries zones had been established.

The illegal drug war had begun in earnest in the Caribbean as the producers of cocaine and marijuana began to expand their markets northward into major metropolitan areas of the United States. What was once considered a minor habit of the dreaded "dope fiends" were now recreational drugs for millions who paid ever-increasing prices for "product." Drug traffickers attempted air, land, and sea transport, but the sea afforded the greatest opportunity. Thus, the Coast Guard found itself fighting a quiet war against smugglers. At first, it was touch-and-go as the smugglers had the resources and money to buy whatever it took to get their deadly product into the United States, which regrettably represent over 80 percent of their users and revenue source. Slowly, the Coast Guard began to fight back and clamp an iron shield around the United States. As the Coast Guard continues to take advantage of electronic systems and new Integrated Deepwater Project assets, smugglers will find it increasingly difficult to get their merchandise into the United States.

Aside from drug smuggling and the Cold War with the Soviet bloc, thousands of refugees attempted to gain illegal access to the United States via boats, rafts, inner tubes, and anything else that could float. The Coast Guard had to save these people and either bring them to the United States or return them to their home country.

September 11, 2001 is a day that Americans will never forget. Thousands were killed when four terrorist-commandeered commercial aircraft slammed into the World Trade Center twin towers in New York City; the Pentagon in Arlington, Virginia; and a farm field in Pennsylvania. Americans now had to look over their shoulder, even in their own country. An effective way to protect the United States in the future was to create a Department of Homeland Security, in which several federal agencies were combined with similar goals and mandates. The U.S. Coast Guard became one of the lead agencies and was transferred to its new department on March 1, 2003. The Coast Guard is now responsible for guarding our shores from unknown and unseen enemies. It is a difficult task, but sharing information with other agencies as well as receiving additional funding for the Integrated Deepwater Project will be helpful.

The cutter *Roger B. Taney* is preserved in Baltimore Harbor as a museum ship. The cutter fought in the attack on Pearl Harbor on December 7, 1941. *Author's Collection*

3 U.S. Coast Guard in Wartime—National Defense

The United States, as a maritime nation, required more than a few small Revenue cutters to protect its shores, collect taxes, prevent smuggling, and perform a myriad of other duties. The Revenue Marine Service and the carryover of British colonial status afforded some protection against foreign enemies.

The greatest challenge was yet to come—the Civil War over economics, slavery, and the ultimate abolition of the feudal system in the South. Wars fought on domestic soil are always the bloodiest and remain the longest in memory. In the Civil War, the Revenue Service found itself on both sides of the fence.

War Between Brothers: The American Civil War

Prior to the beginning of the war in April 1861, the Revenue Marine or Revenue Cutters were transferred to the U.S. Navy or were retained by Confederate sympathizers in southern ports. Many Revenue Marine officers and ratings remained with their home states despite the admonition several decades before by Alexander Hamilton that no officer should become too attached to any particular geographical area. However, even those who were assigned to cutters operating out of northern ports often had to make the decision between defending their home state or their country. Those first few months were quite difficult for many officers who had to choose.

A commission in the Confederate Navy or the role as a shareholder of a blockade runner serving in one's home state was attractive. It was also disloyal, and at war's end, ended any prospect for further employment in the Revenue Marine. A blockade runner is the antithesis of a Revenue Cutter. One is sworn to avoid the other, and the Revenue Cutter is sworn to seize or destroy the blockade runner.

As a matter of irony, the first formal shot of the Civil War was fired by the former Revenue Cutter USS *Harriet Lane* when she fired over the bow of the flagless SS *Nashville*. The *Nashville* did not respond, but the shore batteries opened fire at 4:30 A.M. on Fort Sumter. Fortuitously, no blood was shed, despite over 3,000 shells being fired. The uncontrolled cheering died down in the streets of Charleston, and then reality began to sink in.

It was all for naught as Anderson surrendered, and what was left of his command embarked on the SS *Baltic* and sailed with the other ships northward. The *Baltic* went on to New York where Anderson was feted as a hero.

The *Lane* fought bravely during the war. It ran aground once on August 29, 1861 and became the flagship for Commander David D. Porter's mortar flotilla that wrought havoc on Confederate ground forces on inland waters (the Mississippi River). The *Lane* captured the Confederate vessel *Joanna Ward* during a

The U.S. Revenue cutter *Harriet Lane* firing over the steamship *Nashville* as it races toward Charleston, South Carolina, harbor for refuge in 1861. The *Harriet Lane* and other Revenue cutters that remained in the Union cause acquitted themselves in the American Civil War. *USCG*

spirited battle and chase off the Florida coast, but the revenue-cutter-turned-warship was captured on January 1, 1863 when it was trapped in Galveston Bay. The Confederate Army and naval forces fought the ship until almost all of the members aboard, including the captain and executive officer, were killed. The Confederate government renamed the ship the CSS *Lavinia*, and to add insult to injury, refitted the ex-revenue cutter as a blockade runner. The South was desperate for goods and supplies from Europe, so it would take a chance on any deepwater craft. However, this role was never fulfilled, and soon after it was seized, the metamorphosed vessel escaped to Havana, Cuba, where it was interned until war's end. At that time, she was sold to a commercial interest and was renamed the SS *Elliott Richie*.

By 1884, time and technology had rendered the ship obsolete. She was abandoned in a ship graveyard in Pernambuco, Brazil on May 13, 1884.

Spanish-American War

The Spanish-American War involved the future elements of the Coast Guard in a number of different ways. Many of the lifesaving stations employed the surf men and lighthouse keepers as coast watchers to guard against attack by the Spanish on American soil. This never occurred, but there was an effective beach patrol that formed a precedent for World Wars I and II, when Coast Guard personnel patrolled the beaches with large canines and on horseback seeking Japanese or German saboteurs and U-boats.

The cutter *Ossipee* was one of six cutters transferred to the U.S. Navy during World War I. Five of the six cutters returned. The *Tampa* was sunk by a submarine-launched torpedo just weeks before the armistice. *USCG*

The Spanish Navy was built on imagery and pride, whereas the emerging U.S. Navy was made of steel and a desire to win. The Revenue Cutter Service made some contributions during this short war. One of the cutters, the USRC *McCulloch,* accompanied Admiral Dewey into Manila Bay, Philippines. The *McCulloch* was not needed in the gun line that decimated the Spanish fleet stationed in the Philippines, but was later employed as a dispatch boat and supplementary escort for troop ships.

On the other side of the globe in Caribbean waters on May 11, 1898, the *Hudson*, an armed tug that was also a Revenue Cutter, distinguished itself and entered the battle at Cardenas Bay to protect the wounded torpedo boat USS *Winslow*, which was under the command of Lieutenant John B. Bernadou.

Without hesitation, the *Hudson* rescued the damaged torpedo boat and shot its way out of danger. The *Winslow* had to be towed at the last moment by the *Hudson*. The officers and men of the *Hudson* were decorated for their bravery by Congress. Lieutenant Frank Newcomb, USRCS, received a gold medal for his courage under fire, and a silver medal was awarded to all of the other officers. All of the crewmembers were awarded bronze medals for their bravery.

World War I

World War I witnessed the loss of one of the favorite vessels in the newly formed U.S. Coast Guard. The cutter *Tampa* was sunk by a German U-boat on September 26, 1918, just weeks before the armistice. The *Tampa* had been one of six vessels transferred from the Coast Guard to U.S. Navy control and sent to the European theater of operations. Among these vessels, they destroyed several *U-boats* and ensured that many others were unable to torpedo their prey. When the *Tampa* was lost, she went down with all 131 men on board. The *Tampa* had escorted 18 convoys totaling 350 valuable, defenseless ships and lost only 2 in a grueling area of the overall war zone.

Coast Guard cutters were not really suited for antisubmarine warfare, but the presence of a warship frequently served as a deterrent to U-boats that preyed mainly on unaccompanied or broken-down ships.

During World War I, 8,835 men served in the Coast Guard, and 660 men who belonged to the services that became the Coast Guard fought in the Spanish-American War.

The cutter *Roger B. Taney* is preserved in Baltimore Harbor as a museum ship. The cutter fought in the attack on Pearl Harbor on December 7, 1941. *Author's Collection*

World War II

World War II began in September 1939 for the United States with a need for beefed up port security. U.S. government leaders quickly realized that a world war would eventually include the U.S., and that our harbors and ports would require additional safekeeping. The Coast Guard was the logical and legitimate force for this task.

The Coast Guard began to seize ships in American harbors that were thought to be dangerous or laden with explosives or contraband. In March 1941, the Coast Guard seized and retained 2 German, 28 Italian, 35 Danish cargo, and other vessels. The United Kingdom was so desperate for any type of ship that could

Landing ships, tanks, and other vessels crowd a staging area for the Normandy invasion during World War II. Many of these craft were manned by men of the Coast Guard, including a large number of 83-foot rescue craft that led some of the amphibious ships in the invasion. *Author's Collection*

serve as a convoy escort that the Coast Guard voluntarily transferred 10 relatively modern large cutters to the Royal Navy under the provisions of the Lend Lease Act. This was achieved days after potentially dangerous vessels were seized in American harbors.

Next, the Coast Guard found itself in Greenland. Greenland was the state property of Denmark, which had already fallen to the Nazis, and it behooved the United States to protect Greenland and Iceland. In this respect, Coast Guard personnel from the cutter

U.S. Coast Guard cutter *Campbell* (WHEC-32), sister to the *Taney* and a *Treasury*-class cutter from 1936. For over 50 years, these craft fought the enemies of the United States, including fishing poachers in the North Pacific. They were based on the *Erie*-class U.S. Navy gunboat/cruisers that were unsuitable for naval work, but almost ideal for USCG operations. *USCG*

Northland took the *Boskoe*, a Norwegian trawler, and its three German meteorologists into protective custody on September 12, 1941. They were radioing weather information back to German air and naval bases that enabled

their forces to attack vital convoys en route to Russia and Great Britain. This was the first capture of enemy personnel during the war.

The war claimed the lives of 574 Coast Guard members out of the 241,093 who had

The Korean War made little demand on the USCG; however, several new destroyer escorts were loaned to the Coast Guard from the reserve fleets and painted white for USCG operations. Here is the USCG cutter *Lowe* (W-425). As the USCG built its own vessels, which were primarily for inshore work, they returned the destroyer escorts to the Navy. *USCG*

A USCG *Point*-class patrol boat is on duty in Vietnamese waters. At one time, there were five 311-foot cutters and 26 of the *Point* class assigned to the area. Many of the 82-footers made it back to the United States before they were captured by the North Vietnamese. Today, there are no more active *Point*-class vessels in the USCG, but they can be seen on patrol as part of the maritime forces of other nations. *USCG*

joined up. The men and women of the Coast Guard sank 11 German U-boats from surface ships and one from a Coast Guard aircraft. They rescued men in the water in an 83-foot rescue craft during the D-day Normandy invasion and manned landing craft, landing ship tanks (LSTs), and landing ship infantry (LCIs) throughout the world. The Coast Guard was present at every important invasion during the war, and one of its coxswain's, Signalman First Class Douglas A. Munro, was posthumously awarded the Congressional Medal of Honor for bravery during the Solomons Campaign. Another 2,000 Coast Guard members were awarded citations for bravery and courage under fire.

Korean and Vietnam Wars

The Coast Guard was employed in both the Korean and Vietnam Wars. During the Korean War, the Coast Guard spent much of its effort in port security, harbor protection, and ammunition handling. In the Vietnam War, 26 of the 82-foot *Point*-class patrol boats were deployed to Southeast Asia to interdict Vietcong and enemy supplies and contraband transported on the extensive waterway system. Of the 8,000 men assigned to Vietnam, seven were lost. But the work performed by the *Point* class helped reduce the flow of supplies.

Persian Gulf and Tanker Wars

Water temperature: 80-plus degrees. Blowing sand and dust. Temperatures over 110 degrees with maximum humidity. The conditions were miserable and the odor of crude oil hung heavy in the air. Clumps of unrefined crude oil floated everywhere, and beaches were soiled with the waste of the greatest oil-producing region in the world. It was the duty of the U.S. Coast Guard and Navy to guard this supply of energy. The USCG provided aircraft to assess the bio-damage done by the retreating Republican Grand Army and later assessed in Port Security. The Persian Gulf is one of the most polluted areas in the world, and the USCG routinely provides aid, advice, and assistance to reduce oil pollution.

Operation Enduring Freedom

This defense began in earnest on the morning of September 11, 2001, when four commandeered commercial airliners were overtaken by terrorists. Two of the airliners hit the World Trade Center towers in New York, and a third

On September 11, 2001, Coastie Billy Bashaw is captured as he weeps for his friends and nation forever changed forever by terrorism. *USCG*

struck a wing of the Pentagon, headquarters of the Department of Defense. The World Trade Center buildings, which were less than four decades old, toppled, but not before New York City fire, police, and even a few local Coast Guard personnel were able to bravely lead some 25,000 innocent workers out of the buildings to relative safety. Just under 3,000 people perished, and countless others were injured.

On September 13, 2003, two years and two days after the terrorist attacks, a new unit is established by the USCG on Staten Island. It consists of 104 specially trained staff members who can deal with nuclear, biological, and chemical attacks. They are the Maritime and Safety Security Team (MSST) 91106 and are a permanent addition to the immediate area. *USCG*

The aircraft that hit the Pentagon did not kill as many as the two that struck the World Trade Center, but it was clear that all four aircraft-turned-human-guided-missiles were designed to disrupt the American monetary, military, communication, and political leadership systems at their very core.

Within hours of the terrorists attacks on the United States, *Island*-class patrol boats (WPB) and every other asset the Coast Guard could

This is the *Point Brower* in August 2002. The *Point Brower* was one of the two remaining *Point*-class vessels in the USCG in 2002, and now serves in the patrol and coast guard forces of Adjerbazan. She was transported to this small, eastern European nation in early 2003 after being refitted and overhauled in Richmond, California. *Author's Collection*

mobilize was deployed at crucial maritime points around the nation. The job was to guard and protect citizens, structures, harbors, oil depots, and other assets necessary to a maritime nation. The Coast Guard was woefully underfunded and didn't have the necessary resources to provide the type of security necessary to prevent further attacks on American assets. Clearly, more had to be done to ensure the safety of the American people. What was achieved by the U.S. Coast Guard and the U.S. military in the hours and days after the stunning attacks on the homeland of the United States was nothing short of miraculous.

The high-endurance cutter *Dallas* (WHEC-716) escorts the vessel M/VBBC *Spain,* which carries four 110-foot *Island*-class patrol vessels into the Iraqi war zone on March 19, 2003. The cradles for the patrol boats had been built for Operation Desert Storm in 1991, but were not used because the war ended before there was a crucial need for Coast Guard inshore vessels. *USCG*

The Coast Guard could not abandon its overall responsibilities to the public or the international community, so it recalled many reservists and volunteers for a surge operation to provide resources where they were most necessary. Port Security Units (PSU) were comprised of 2,700 reservists and guarded the maritime gates to the nation where the United States could be most vulnerable. The chances of another airliner assault by terrorists was

The high-endurance cutter *Boutwell* (WHEC-719) is in the North Arabian Gulf on May 6, 2003, to provide fuel, food, laundry services, and showers to the crew of the *Island*-class patrol boat tied to her starboard side aft. Generally, the *Boutwell* and other USCG vessels operated alone this far up in the Arabian Gulf because the deep draft of the U.S. Navy's vessels forbade them from inshore work. The exception was the *Cyclone*-class patrol coastal patrol boats and other smaller craft that were used to disperse mines and clear harbors. *USCG*

dimmed by increased security at the nation's airports, but the opportunity for attack from the sea rose to the top of a short list of possible assaults. The U.S. Coast Guard would have to step up to the plate with Port Security Units to watch over major harbor facilities, inspect more of the cargoes of the estimated 8,000 vessels coming and going through U.S. ports, and assist local port officials to secure harbors from unwanted intruders.

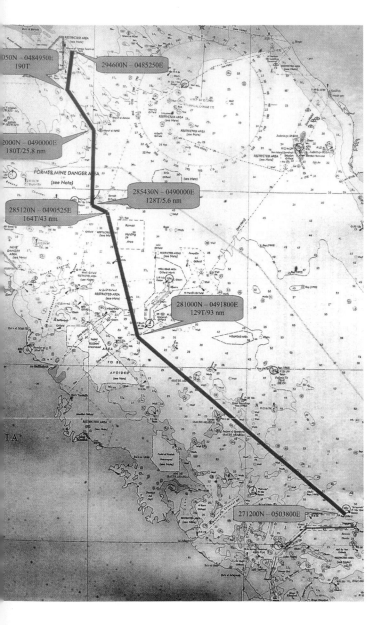

Labels on map:
- 050N – 0484950E / 190T
- 294600N – 0485250E
- 2000N – 0490000E / 180T/25.8 nm
- 285430N – 0490000E / 128T/5.6 nm
- 285120N – 0490525E / 164T/43 nm
- 281000N – 0491800E / 129T/93 nm
- 271200N – 0503800E

A map and instructions are in English and Arabic for all vessels passing through the war zone. The basic idea was to avoid the deaths of innocent people. The Iraqi mariners were grateful. *USCG*

In the immediate wake of the attacks on the World Trade Center, over 1 million New Yorkers were evacuated to safer locations. This meant emergency travel by boat, ferry, commercial tugs, and every Coast Guard craft available. The Coast Guard deployed 55 cutters, 42 available aircraft, and virtually every spare aircraft to patrol U.S. ports and harbors.

On September 12, 2003, the Coast Guard commissioned a Maritime Safety and Security Team (MSST) composed of 104 members who have the expertise to counter chemical, biological, and radiological incidents in the New York/New Jersey area. Team 91106 is based in a high-threat area to prevent or reduce the impact

Merchant vessel, you have been inspected by a Coalition Boarding Team and have been cleared to proceed to your next port of call. The route described below will provide the safest and most expeditious route out of the combat areas. It is recommended that you follow this route so you will be known to Coalition Warships as an uninvolved merchant vessel and no harm will come to you, your vessel or your cargo.

NOTE: If you choose to alter from the navigation track given below you and your vessel may be in danger of being misidentified and possibly subject to coalition defensive measures.

From your present position you will be escorted to 2946N 04852.5E, after which you will be released to proceed wherever you wish.

We recommend, however, that you proceed on the following route:

1. Proceed from the release point on course 190 degrees until you reach 2930.5N-04849.5E.

2. From this point turn southeast toward pt 2920000N-0490000E which is before the "Fairway" Buoy (a quick flashing blue/yellow light).

3. Head south until you get to pt 285430N-0490000E.

4. Turn southeast between Durrah and Hut Oilfields until you arrive at pt 285120N-0490525E.

5. Turn southeast towards buoy "1", a flashing red/white light every 10s until you get to 281000N-0491800E. On your way, you will pass to the west of Buoy "Z1" in position 281500N-0491700E, which has a flashing red light every 3 seconds at the southern exit of AZ ZULUF OILFIELD traffic separation scheme.

6. Continue southeast to point 271200N-0503800E in the vicinity of the JU'AYMAH RACON Buoy, the first of two steady red rotating lights.

7. Proceed to your next port of call. Iraqi ports are closed until further notice. If you intend to return to a port in Kuwait or Iran, it is recommended you follow the navigation track above on your return.

Departing S.A.A (IRAN)

ADVISEMENT: You will encounter coalition warshi[ps] route. If you are challenged by a Coalition warship, r[eport your] vessel name and the serial number on your clearance [paper.] Should you deviate from this route, it is likely that yo[u will be] boarded again. Coalition forces strongly urge you to [follow this] route precisely to avoid being mistaken for the enem[y. Your] cooperation is appreciated.

سفن خلاف حرية في هذا الطريق. اذا نادت هذه السفن عليكم اجبروا الفداء باسم
السفل الموجود على اورظالضريج الرسمي. اذا خوفم من مسوكم فسيكون من الضمل
مرة اخرى ان قوى الاتلاف ترجوا منكم ان تباعوا هذا الطريق حتى لا تعبركم عدو.

Ship Name_____ Serial #___

Issuing Officer _____

Date _____ Time _____

of weapons of mass destruction entering the nation via the sea.

Incorporating Sea Marshals was another safety tactic. As early as February 2002, armed and highly trained Sea Marshals were available to board and inspect passenger and commercial vessels. They are trained in law enforcement and give passengers a sense of protection not afforded by the cruise lines. In addition, the USCG established the Marine Safety and Security Team concept, which is much like the Port Security Unit, but takes a proactive stance to harbor security by boarding and searching suspicious vessels and conducting random searches. The Coast Guard also established and enforced a 500-yard security zone (Naval Vessel Protection Zone) around all navy ships, whether moored, anchored, or in transit.

Foreign and domestic ships entering U.S. waters are now required to provide a 96-hour advance notice. The vessels must report their arrival and departure to the National Vessel Movement Center. This is vital to regulate traffic and help prevent unwanted or suspicious vessels from entering U.S. ports.

The overall response to the attacks on September 11, 2001 by the U.S. Coast Guard has led to many important and valuable changes in the way the service operates and protects the United States from enemies that might try to enter the country by sea. The new ways of doing business are simply to detect a new type of enemy who will sacrifice themselves for a purpose. It is a war of those who seek to live versus those who seek to die.

In essence, the Coast Guard works more closely with the U.S. Navy than ever before. Although, Operation Enduring Freedom is

This is an Iraqi oil platform in the Northern northern Arabian Gulf. It is known as the Khawr al Amaja oil terminal, and is likely working again. One terminal was reputed to have soldiers, RPGs, and other heavy weapons. The *Boutwell* warned the platform of SEALs and other forces coming. The Iraqis surrendered and the explosives were disconnected. In the background, the *Boutwell* steamed at slow speed with its lookouts searching for anything that might strike the hull. *USCG*

On April 20, 2003, a boarding term team from the cutter *Boutwell* has just examined the craft in the background and will search for contraband and dangers to coalition forces elsewhere. *USCG*

technically a war on a global scale, it is not considered a war similar to World War I or World War II, when the U.S. Coast Guard was seconded to the Navy Department. Operation Enduring Freedom requires a shared approach to victory. The Coast Guard takes up the charge of homeland defense at the sea approaches to the U.S., and the U.S. Navy does what is necessary to take on the war in foreign lands. This does not mean the specialized skills and assets of the Coast Guard will be solely confined to American waters. The Coast Guard has been required to act in the successful war to free Iraq from the grasp of Saddam Hussein and the Ba'ath Party.

The British Royal Fleet Auxiliary (RFA) ship *Sir Galahad* sails up the Khawr Allah River on March 28, 2003, to the port of Umm Qsar Qasr to discharge its 4,000 tons of cargo—much of it for humanitarian purposes. The *Sir Galahad* is escorted by USCG *Raider* craft and *Island*-class patrol boats. *USCG*

The service was also involved in supporting NATO operations in Kosovo and assisted at Guantanamo Bay and in operations in Haiti in 1994. Its most recent and prominent role has been in the Persian Gulf to help liberate Iraq.

Operation Iraqi Freedom

In early 2003, the Coast Guard deployed eight 110-foot *Island*-class patrol craft and two Port Security Units with a total of 600 Coast Guard men and women in support of Operation

On May 24, 2003, a USCG Coast Guard LEDET rides on a U.S. Navy rubber raiding craft from the patrol coastal boat USS *Chinook* (PC-9) on its way to examine a sunken derelict near the port of Umm Qasr. The USCG team is from the *Island*-class patrol boat *Aquidneck* (WPB-1309). There were rumors that pro-Saddam Hussein irregulars were holed up in the wreck that and were laying mines at night. The team went to the wreck to clear them out and make the port safe for traffic. *USCG*

Enduring Freedom. The *Adak, Wrangell, Grand Isle, Bainbridge Island, Aquidneck, Baranof, Knight Island,* and *Pea Island* patrol boats were sent abroad for Operation Iraqi Freedom. The high-endurance cutter *Boutwell* (WHEC-719), based at

Coast Guard Island in Alameda, California, received similar orders to deploy to the Persian Gulf. The foreign contingent also included a six-member specialist team (National Strike Force) in maritime pollution response in case the Iraqi regime decided to attack with crude oil spills and burning oil heads. The team was housed aboard the relatively modern *Juniper*-class, 225-foot seagoing buoy tender *Walnut* (WLB-205), previously assigned to Hawaiian waters. This craft's ATON crew of specialists went from paradise to misery within a month due to blowing sand, excessive outdoor heat, high water temperature, and other wartime conditions.

Operation Enduring Freedom can mean many things to many people, but to the Coast Guard, it means being where it is needed to respond to this new twenty-first century form of warfare to protect American citizens and port facilities. In the early hours of March 20, 2003, the U.S. Navy cruisers USS *Cowpens* (CG-63), USS *Bunker Hill* (CG-52), destroyers USS *Milius* (DDG-69), USS *Donald Cook* (DDG-75), and improved *Los Angeles*-class submarines USS *Montpelier* (SSN-765) and USS *Cheyenne* (SSN-773), launched a series of Tomahawk land-attack missiles to complement those fired by a U.S. Air Force F-117A Nighthawk stealth aircraft. The target was a suspected meeting location in downtown Baghdad, Iraq where Saddam Hussein, his sons, and party worthies were thought to be meeting. Many of the leaders were killed, and the war to free Iraq from the regime of this dictator began.

The Coast Guard deployed over 1,200 men and women to the Northern Arabian Gulf theater of operations. The deployment included two 378-foot high-endurance cutters, the *Boutwell* and *Dallas*, the 270-foot medium-endurance cutter *Spencer*, the 225-foot seagoing buoy tender *Walnut,* and eight 110-foot *Island*-class patrol boats. Also included were mobile support units (MSUs), law

On April 19, 2003, the ocean-going buoy tender, *Walnut,* is almost framed by an Iraqi ATON, which will probably need work to help guide ships up the Khawr Abd Allah waterway and the port of Umm Qasr. Before its repairs, the ship will be searched for mines. This is a routine procedure because the mines and explosive obstructions would could have killed or maimed innocent Coasties. *USCG*

At Nauticus, near Norfolk, Virginia, the *Island*-class boats *Grand Isle, Pea Island, Bainbridge Island, Knight Island,* and the high-endurance cutter *Dallas* are greeted by families and friends on June 11, 2003. Four other *Island*-class boats remain at work in the war zone, but they will come home soon. The Coast Guard and its vessels proved the worth of the littoral warfare vessel. *USCG*

enforcement detachments (LEDETs), port security units (PSUs), and a national strike force to deal with oil spills and fires.

The *Boutwell* and *Dallas* had to serve as mother ships to the 110-foot *Island*-class boats

that could not produce their own water and had limited range.

As the war continued, the humidity grew with the heat, rain, and dust storms that blew over the northern Arabian gulf. Almost every inch of the vessels was covered with dirt, mud, and dust. There has been continuous difficulty with the belligerency of the Iranians, who taunted the Coast Guard with high-speed Swedish-built patrol boats day and night. The Iranians threatened the patrol boats and larger 378s with rocket-propelled grenades, as well as a myriad of other weapons. The U.S. Navy rarely ventured far up into the areas where the Coast Guard could go, due to too deep of a draft, so it was up to the Guard and some of the older patrol coastal boats of the *Cyclone* class to carry the load. Lookouts were posted at points all around the ships to search for mines, sand bars, and other floating obstacles. The intakes were often fouled with sand or huge flows of jellyfish that appeared from nowhere.

In general, the Iraqi people were happy to see the American Coast Guard, but the primary threat came from nightly drops of floating mines or the Iranian navy that came out to pester the Coast Guard. They would shout obscenities and threats, but left when they felt that they might be on the receiving end of 76mm shells or torn apart by the *Boutwell*'s close-in weapons system (CIWS).

The seagoing buoy tender *Walnut* performed magnificently and repaired or replaced dozens of faulty aids to navigation to allow shipping access to ports in southern Iraq, and the Port Security Units (PSUs) protected the newly freed harbors and oil drilling platforms. The PSUs employed *Raider* patrol boats to watch over the harbors and ports on a continuous basis.

In June 2003, the war came to an end for the first units of the Coast Guard assigned to Operation Iraqi Freedom. A small force of four *Island* class Coast Guard patrol craft still remain, and although they are considered the enemy, they are not out for destruction. Most of the people realize that the white boats with the slashes on their sides are friendly until provoked.

Three HC-130 Hercules sit on the line at the Sacramento Coast Guard Air Station and await mission instructions. *Author's Collection*

4 Vessels, Patrol/Utility Boats, and Aircrafts

Currently, the U.S. Coast Guard has several major vessels and aircraft available to meet their missions. There are 12 *Hamilton*-class, deep-draft, high-endurance, 378-foot-long cutters. These vessels were originally built from the late 1960s to the early 1970s. They displace 3,300 tons full load and have been modified through a fleet rehabilitation and modernization program (FRAM) from 1985 to 1992. The cutters are capable of 29 knots on their combined gas turbine and diesel power plants and carry a mixed crew of 167 men and women. The *Hamilton* class is armed with one Mark 75 76mm gun that can fire up to 80 rounds in quick and rapid succession. They also carry a rapid-fire Gatling gun, 20mm Vulcan Phalanx CIWS aft, and two Mark 38 Bushmaster chain 25mm machine guns located on each side amid ships. There are also two .50-caliber machine guns and numerous small arms, as well as a single Jayhawk or Dolphin helicopter that can either be a variant. This class also carries the SUBROC capability for ASW warfare. The 378 is employed in about every mission the Coast Guard has to offer and is the single largest asset in the service's inventory. The recent war in Iraq required the cutter *Boutwell* (WHEC–719), based out of Alameda's Coast Guard Island, to act as flagship for a number of smaller patrol boats and a modern *Juniper*-class ocean-going buoy tender, the *Walnut* (WLB-205). The *Boutwell* and its replacement, the *Dallas* (WHEC–716), performed without any major breakdowns and were a credit to the coalition forces that defeated Saddam Hussein's military regime.

There are 13 *Bear*-or *Famous*-class medium-endurance 270-foot-long cutters. These cutters began with the inaugural vessel, the *Bear* (WMEC-901), which entered service in 1983 and is based in Portsmouth, Virginia. This type of ship displaces 1,820 tons full load with a top speed of 19.5 knots on two diesels with 7,300 brake horsepower. Like their larger sisters in the *Hamilton* class, they carry a single 76mm gun and .50-caliber machine guns, as well as submarine rocket (SUBROC) launchers for ASW work. Their complement can include up to 100 men and women, and they can carry a Dolphin, Jayhawk, or Mako (Stingray) helicopter.

Another class of medium-endurance cutter is the *Reliance,* which is 210 feet in length and displaces 1,020 tons full load. There are 16 cutters in this class, and they are powered by twin diesels generating 5,000 brake horsepower. They have maximum speed of 18 knots and carry a crew of 75. The *Reliance* class is armed with a single Mark 38 25mm Bushmaster gun, two .50-caliber guns, and other small arms. Like their bigger sisters, they can embark a Dolphin or Mako helicopter.

Three *Hamilton*-class cutters are in port at Coast Guard Island in October 2003. From right to left are the *Boutwell* (WHEC-719), *Munro* (WHEC-724), and *Sherman* (WHEC-724). The *Boutwell* has been home ported in Seattle, Washington; Boston, Massachusetts; and now, Alameda, California. *Author's Collection*

The Coast Guard has a number of vessels, such as the medium-endurance-class cutter *Storis* (WMEC-38), that were built 61 years ago. The *Storis* operates primarily in the northern reaches of the United States and displaces 1,920 tons on her 230 feet of length. Her base is in Kodiak, Alaska, the home of the medium-endurance cutter *Alex Haley* (WMEC-39), which has a 3,000-ton displacement and is 282 feet in length. The last of the older vessels is the *Acushnet*

(WMEC-167) of the U.S. Navy's *Diver* class. Based out of Ketchikan, Alaska, the *Acushnet* was built during World War II for the Navy. Many of the sister ships are being used in commercial ventures and can be seen in the backwaters of various harbors. All of these isolated ships are in very good condition, but are incapable of further upgrades. All need to be replaced with modern equipment and electronics, which will occur with the Integrated Deepwater Project.

The *Reliance*-class cutter *Steadfast* (MWEC-623) is escorted by a bevy of craft and a *Jayhawk* helicopter as it sails up the Columbia River. The *Reliance* class tops out at 1,020 tons full load and can transport a helicopter. *USCG*

The ocean-going buoy tender *Walnut* (WLB-305) tends the last of the buoys leading up to Iraq's best and most accessible port, Umm Qasr, on May 5, 2003. Along the 41-mile stretch of inland water, the *Walnut* replaced 30 and repaired 5 buoys.

The 49 110-foot *Island*-class patrol boats are roughly based on a very successful British-designed craft and have become the backbone of the Coast Guard's mosquito fleet of vessels. They are attractive, well founded, and at 154 tons full load, have proven that they can sail across the Atlantic and the Mediterranean when needed for war. They carry a crew of 16 and are built on an assembly line by Bollinger Machine Shop and Shipyard in Lockport, Louisiana. They do not have the creature comforts of larger vessels, but they are handsome and near perfect for the roles laid out for them. Under the plan to improve the Coast Guard's ability to carry out homeland security, the *Island*-class patrol boat *Matagorda* (WPB-1303), based out of Miami Beach, Florida, has been decommissioned for reconstruction by Bollinger to add 13 feet to its stern. The purpose is to accommodate a stern gate to launch a rigid-hull inflatable or *Over the Horizon* interdiction craft. If the prototype is successful, revamps to other *Island*-class vessels will follow. The current *Island* class is armed with a single Mark 38 25mm Bushmaster chain gun, two .50-caliber machine guns with shields, and a variety of other small arms. This class is based in harbors and ports all along the coasts of the United States and its possessions. The *Island* class is diesel powered with a top speed of 29.5 knots and a range of 1,900 miles.

The 51 Marine Protector-class *Barracuda*, 87-foot patrol boats are 91 tons full load and can make up to 25 knots on their twin diesel engines. Armed with two .50-caliber machine guns, these craft can be found in smaller ports and carry a rigid-hull inflatable aft with a stern gate, which preceded those on the *Cyclone* class of Navy coastal patrol boats by several years. Thirteen more of these craft are slated for the Coast Guard in the next year. Their popularity extends to the Maltese Maritime Squadron's *P-51* variant, which is 87 feet long and displaces 91.1 tons full load with a maximum range of 882 miles and top speed of 27 knots. The influence of British design is unmistakable in the *Marine Protector* class, the Maltese *P-51,* and the 110-foot *Island* class.

The U.S. Coast Guard has four major icebreakers. The *Polar* class includes the *Polar Star* (WAGB-10) and the *Polar Sea* (WAGB-11), which are based out of Seattle, Washington. They are each 13,100 tons full load and 399 feet in length. They are powered with 60,600 shaft horsepower from 3 gas turbines and 3 diesel engines. Their range is 28,000 miles, and they carry a mixed crew of up to 170 members,

A cold snap in Washington, D.C., requires a Coast Guard icebreaker to free and guide barges up the river. Here the *Gentian* (WLB-290) of the *Balsam* class assists, with the Washington Monument in the background. The *Gentian* is one of the few vessels of her aging class to survive. It is now painted white and is serving in the Caribbean. *USCG*

This is a rare view of one of the remaining 52-foot motor life boats stationed at Cape Disappointment in Ilwaco, Washington. Four of these wooden craft were built in 1962 and cost $236,000 each. They have a top speed of 11 knots from a 2,170 horsepower GM diesel. *Author's Collection*

including scientists and research technicians. Both are capable of embarking two *Dolphin* or *Jayhawk* helicopters that are housed in permanent hangars. Both vessels are over 25 years old. The other two major icebreakers are

the *Healy* (WAGB-20) and the *Mackinaw* (WAGB-83). The *Healy* displaces 16,400 tons, is 420 feet in length, and has a top speed of 17 knots on 4 diesels generating 30,000 shaft horsepower. The *Healy* embarks two *Dolphins* or one *Dolphin* and one *Jayhawk* helicopter and can carry a crew of 120, including 45 scientific research crew. The *Mackinaw* is the oldest of the icebreakers and operates on the Great Lakes. She was commissioned in 1944 and will have served for 61 years when she's replaced in 2005. The 5,252-ton full load icebreaker is 290 feet in length and is capable of 18.7 knots on 6 diesels generating 10,000 shaft horsepower. The *Mackinaw's* homeport is Cheboygan, Michigan, and her crew consists of 75 men and women. The *Mackinaw,* which began as the *Manitowoc,* has freed ships and plowed pathways through the ice for other vessels to ensure that commerce continues unabated.

The Coast Guard also employs seagoing (*Juniper, Balsam* classes) and coastal (*Keeper* class) buoy tenders, inland buoy tenders (100 and 65 feet), construction and river tenders (100, 160, and 75 feet), and 627 small harbor craft including SAR and rigid-hull inflatable boats.

U.S. Coast Guard Aircraft

It is almost impossible to envision a Coast Guard without aircraft to carry out its missions. The introduction of aircraft into the Coast Guard came directly after the Coast Guard's formation in 1915. On August 29, 1916, Congress authorized 10 Coast Guard air stations and equipment including aero planes. This never came to fruition due to the onset of World War I and the transfer of the newly formed federal agency to the Navy Department. Of course, after the war ended in 1918, the Coast Guard attempted to assert its rights to previous allocations, but was only allowed the temporary use of the Naval Air Station at Moorhead City,

The 91-ton *Marine Protector*-class *Cormorant* (WPB-87313) is at sea with its rigid-hull craft aft behind a stern gate. The *Marine Protector* class replaced the *Point* class and travels up to 25 knots on two diesels. *USCG*

North Carolina, and six broken-down, surplus HS-2L flying boats. By 1920, the entire Coast Guard air operation had gone bankrupt and remained so until 1924.

PREVIOUS PAGES: The *Island*-class patrol boat *Baranof Island* was deployed to the Iraqi war and worked closely with the *Boutwell*. The *Island* class has a 2,400-mile range and can travel up to 29.5 miles per hour. They top 154 tons full load and are heavily armed. The *Baranof* (WPB-1318) is shown patrolling off the Khawr al Amaya oil terminal on May 7, 2003. The *Baranof* provided offshore gunfire support if necessary. *USCG*

In 1924, Lieutenant Commander C. C. von Paulsen borrowed a Vought-produced *UO-1* aircraft from the U.S. Navy and purchased a surplus U.S. Army tent hangar for $1 per year. To show how financially stricken the entire operation was, the Department of Fisheries took pity on von Paulsen and his eager aviator wannabes and permitted them to use an island in Gloucester Harbor, Massachusetts for a base. Twelve months later, the plane had to be returned to the Navy, and the facility was closed.

Finally, on March 3, 1926, appropriations were made available by a congressional act to provide five new airplanes and two Coast Guard air stations. The planes had to be purchased under U.S. Navy contracts and inspected by naval aviators, but it was a start. The first aircraft purchased were Loening OL-5s, which were kept in service until 1935. The HS-2L was the first aircraft flown by Coast Guard aviators, and the Loening OL-5 was the first aircraft actually owned and operated by the Coast Guard.

From this point forward, the aircraft flown by the Coast Guard consisted of castoffs from the U.S. Army and Navy. The Coast Guard name found its way onto used World War II-vintage B-17 Flying Fortresses, B-24 Liberators, Privateers, seaplanes, and anything else that

could fly. The U.S. Air Force-designed C-130 Hercules is still flown by all of the services and is the primary fixed-wing aircraft of the Coast Guard. The Jayhawk is a derivative of the Navy's Sea Hawk.

In the early twenty-first century, there are a number of Coast Guard air stations, but far from what is needed for the diversity of missions this organization finds itself being called upon to carry out. Virtually every cutter carries or can embark a helicopter as a force multiplier.

Primary Fixed-Wing Aircraft

The HC130H Hercules long-range aircraft or the C-130 Hercules are called "Hercs" or "thundering pigs." Of the 27 aircraft, at least 5 are grounded for routine maintenance and stealing parts from other aircraft that the Navy or Air Force has cast off. These aircraft fly at a top speed of over 300 knots and cruise at 280 knots. They have a 132.6-foot wingspan and are 99.6 feet in length with a maximum gross weight of 155,000 pounds. Their range is between 2,500 and 4,400 miles depending on payload and mission configuration. They have four reliable Allison T-56 engines with four blades and carry a crew of two pilots, a flight engineer, navigator, radio operator, dropmaster, and loadmaster. The original design for the C-130 originated 40 years ago for the U.S. Air Force and has metamorphosed through a number of variants. The latest variation intended for the Coast Guard is the C-130J with fully integrated digital avionics, heads-up displays, global positioning systems, and new Rolls-Royce turboprop engines with six-blade composite propellers. The payload will be greater, have more overall power, and the range

A 25-foot *Defender*-class response boat is shown on a trailer near Coast Guard Island in late October 2003. Over 700 of these twin-outboard-engine craft were built. The Coast Guard's new Maritime Safety and Security Teams (MSST) will use them for port security. *Author's Collection*

A rigid-hull inflatable boat (RHIB) is moored in front of a 47-foot surf boat at the Noyo Harbor Coast Guard Station at Fort Bragg, California. The Coast Guard spends much of its time saving lives with its two 47-foot boats and the RHIBs. *Author's Collection by Hunter Lanzaro*

will be far greater than earlier models. The stern ramp opens so rescue equipment can be dispersed to those in the water. The CASA EADS twin-engine maritime-patrol aircraft that is produced in Europe may be added to the fixed-wing inventory. It has gained immense popularity with many air forces and coastal patrols in Europe, Asia, and Ireland.

The Guardian or HU-25 is a medium-range, search-and-rescue, rotary-wing aircraft used by the Coast Guard to perform SAR missions. One of its primary values is its ability to get to a disaster scene quickly, and with an extensive fuel supply it can loiter over a scene for up to four hours. Seventeen of these aircraft are in the Coast Guard inventory and many can now perform more than just SAR missions. The addition of updated electronics has enabled them to carry out a variety of missions and tasks. They have a range of 2,000 miles and a cruise speed of 450 knots on two Garrett ATF-3 turbofan engines. Up to five personnel can be carried aboard these aircraft, depending on the mission.

Rotary-Wing Aircraft Evolution

Rotary-wing aircraft entered service in the U.S. Coast Guard before any branch of the U.S. military. This occurred during the later part of World War II when Sikorsky HSS-1 and HOS-1 helicopters were flown from a makeshift plywood rocking platform on the ground and from the deck of the ancient cutter *Cobb*. The ex-SS *Governor Cobb* was a coastal steamer built in 1906 and confiscated during World War II as the USCG *Cutter Cobb* (WPB-181). The first helicopters were launched and recovered during experiments from its aft platform. At

The *Marine Protector*-class patrol boat *Tern* is moored at the Coast Guard base at Yerba Buena Island in San Francisco Bay. This facility is one of the busiest in the nation. *Author's Collection*

These two 41-foot utility boats were built at the Coast Guard Yard during the 1960s and 1970s. This type of boat has haves been the workhorse for the USCG, and over 100 have been built. They are primarily employed as SAR craft in moderately heavy seas and can accommodate 22 survivors. *Author's Collection*

A utility tug is used as a service aid to navigation in harbors along with many other tasks. Its gantries on the stern are used to lifting medium and lightweight boats and ATONS for repair. *USCG*

first, the Navy and other services saw this as a joke. Little did they know that these canvas-covered rotary-type flying machines combined with ships would hold the future for naval warfare and army troop insertion. They also serve as a means to rescue people at sea, in the mountains, and those lost or in rivers and lakes inaccessible to any other method of rescue.

Not long after the war ended, Coast Guard helicopters began to carry out search-and-rescue missions. Various types of helicopters were employed, and by the end of the twentieth century, the Coast Guard utilized three basic types: the HH-60J Jayhawk, the HH-65A Dolphin or Dauphin, and the MH-68A Stingray. The Stingray is the result of many

trials, and to date, has been deemed the best rotary-wing aircraft for illegal-drug and homeland-security missions. All of the helos have their purposes, and all can be launched and recovered from cutters.

Primary Rotary-Wing Aircraft

The Jayhawk is probably the most popular helicopter because it is a medium-range recovery or search-and-rescue aircraft. It is a member of the Hawk family of helos, such as the U.S. Navy's Seahawk and the U.S. Army's Blackhawk. It has a range of 300 nautical miles and carries a crew of four: two pilots, a flight mechanic, and a rescue swimmer. It is designed to carry 6 passengers, but has been able to carry 26 in a pinch. It cruises at 146 knots and has a ceiling of 13,000 feet. Forty-two Jayhawks are available nationwide for Coast Guard service, but at least seven are being repaired at any one time. Jayhawks carry two GE turbo-shaft engines. The inventory of Jayhawks allotted to the Coast Guard beginning in 1991 is expected to last until 2014 to 2022, depending on upgrades and replacements.

The Dolphin, or Dauphin, is manufactured by Eurocopter and is usually painted red. Its maximum cruise speed is 165 knots and it is considered a medium-range recovery helicopter. Its range is 400 nautical miles and it carries the same crew as the Jayhawk. The Dolphin has the capability to fly in all types of weather and

This modern Coast Guard *Raider* craft is heavily armed and is employed to board vessels that are likely to fight back. Here, USCG personnel have just inspected a cargo vessel off Iraq. *USCG*

83

Here a push tug gets ready to tow a barge full of plastic ATONs into the Mississippi River for placement. The river is always changing, and the Coast Guard must keep an eye on its new pathways for vessel traffic. *Author's Collection*

has become the USCG's workhorse at 50,000 flight hours annually. There are 96 Dolphins in active service and they are nearly state of the art, which makes them ideal for homeland defense and illegal drug patrols.

There are eight MH-68A Stingray high-speed, drug-interdiction, rotary-wing aircraft.

The Coast Guard shopped around for a helicopter interdiction tactical squadron (HITRON) aircraft to attack and stop illegal drug smugglers and selected the MH-90 Enforcer with an M-240 machine gun. The MH-68A Stingray is becoming the all-weather, high-speed, anti-drug-smuggling air asset of

This is the first Coast Guard aviation group at Naval Air Station in Pensacola, Florida, on March 21, 1917. The USCG aviators went through the same program as naval aviators. This was the class of 1916, but to their dismay, there were few or no planes to fly. *USCG*

Antares, the PJ-1 twin engine seaplane, numbered FLB-52, was built by the General Aviation Company of the 1930s. It became a rescue aircraft and test model for the USCG aviation rescue program. This rare color photo shows the seaplane at its base on Cape May. *Author's Collection*

This is one of the few remaining HU-16E Albatross seaplanes formerly used by the USCG. This one is located in Sacramento. The Coast Guard had 88 aircraft in this class that lasted 35 years. The last of the amphibians was decommissioned on March 10, 1983, at USCG Air Station Cape Cod, Massachussetts. The McClellan Air Museum in Sacramento owns this aircraft. *Author's Collection*

choice employed by the Coast Guard. Stingrays have a maximum speed of 168 knots and a weapons package tied to an electronics system that can disable a go-fast boat. The accuracy with a .50-caliber sniper gun is amazing as it punches holes through the engine or outboard engines of boats at speeds in excess of 60 knots. The idea is to capture the smugglers, seize the product, and disable the boat without harm to anyone. Properly operated, the Stingray can

A crewman on the rear ramp of a C-130 Hercules is about to throw a smoke bomb out of the craft to mark the location where a survival package will be aimed during this practice run. The object is to hit on or near the smoke bomb to simulate a rescue attempt. *Author's Collection by Mary Mesmer*

A USCG Sikorsky HSN-J Hoverfly flies from the Coast Guard Air Station at Floyd Bennett Field in 1943. Following on the heels of the Hoverfly, is a number of rotary-wing aircraft including the HO5S-1, which entered service in 1952 and could transport 2,700 pounds of cargo. *USCG*

89

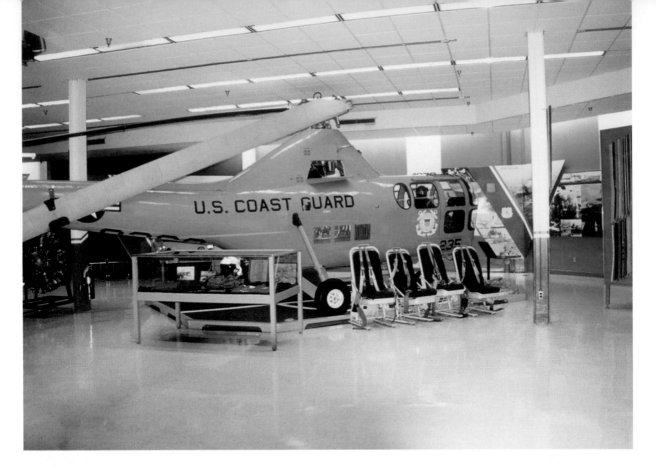

The HO3S flew search-and-rescue missions for the USCG. It also served the U.S. Navy. The example shown here is preserved at the Naval Air Museum in Pensacola, Florida. *Author's Collection*

do this, as can other HITRON aircraft in tandem with cutters and the USCG high-speed over-the-horizon craft.

Aids to Navigation (ATON)

The nation began its aids to navigation program with lighthouses. The Lighthouse Service was one of the first items tackled by the new U.S. Congress and the nation's first president, George Washington. From those early days, the Coast Guard has evolved and now controls over 50,000 various federal aids to navigation with a like number of state and local buoys, lights, fog reflectors, and beacons. These are short-range aids to navigation and, overall, the program consumes 16 to 18 percent of the Coast Guard's budget.

ATONs keep mariners informed of weather and all types of marine information, and the Coast Guard routinely services these aids. Batteries are replaced every 6 to 12 months, and anchor chains that secure the buoys to bottom anchors are routinely cleaned and painted.

Aside from the work that tenders perform, which can be tasks like pulling in miles of unwanted and abandoned fishing netting and

90

An HH-65 Dolphin is aboard the high-endurance cutter *Boutwell* off Iraq during Operation Iraqi Freedom. It is one of the finest aircraft in the Coast Guard inventory. *USCG*

menaces to navigation, shore personnel replace batteries in lighthouses and maintain LORAN-C and the electronic ATONs that have replaced older technologies.

The 24 LORAN-C stations replaced a lot of radio beacon traffic and traditional means of locating a ship's position on the globe, but the latest item to join the family of electronic aids is the global positioning system (GPS). GPS has completely revolutionized lifesaving and position marking. Sailors that are washed overboard now have a fighting chance of survival with a pocket-sized device that sends out a signal to help searchers locate them. In the past, only the sharp eyes of the aft lookout could possibly save a person lost overboard.

An HH-60J Jayhawk all-purpose helicopter is used primarily for SAR from cutters and land bases. It can carry six survivors, but has embarked as many as 26 at the height of a storm. It has the capability of flying 146 knots per hour and up to 13,000 feet. *Author's Collection*

Hundreds of vessels enter and leave U.S. ports each day, and the Coast Guard ensures their safety, as well as the safety of bridges and other structures that straddle the waterways. The ATON program is vital, and the Iraqis and coalition forces found that out early in 2003 in the war against Saddam Hussein. An ocean-going buoy tender, the *Walnut* (WLB-205), had to be sent to replace or repair over 30-year-old buoys and ATONs leading to a port where

The ocean-going buoy tender *Aspen* (WLB-208) sits at her Yerba Buena mooring in San Francisco, California. The *Aspen* is a *Juniper*-class vessel and sister to the *Walnut*, which fought in Operation Iraqi Freedom. *Author's Collection*

ATONs range from lighted buoys to fog and horn buoys. All require constant repair and cleaning on a constant basis. There are over 100,000 ATONs nationwide controlled by various entities, but they still need service and replacement. Some of the repaired ATONs will be taken out to sea by the *Aspen*. *Author's Collection*

humanitarian supplies could be offloaded. Without this, no food or medical assistance could be provided. To make matters worse, most of the old buoys were festooned with explosive mines. Yet, the Coast Guard preserved and the channel leading up the Khawr Abd Allah River was open and relatively safe for shipping traffic. The *Sir Galahad*, of the British RFA (Royal Fleet Auxiliary), was the first ship with humanitarian aid escorted up the channel by Coast Guard *Raider* craft and 110-foot *Island*-class patrol boats.

A Jayhawk makes a mock rescue in San Diego harbor to demonstrate how it and its rescue swimmers retrieve those inpeople from the sea. *Author's Collection*

CHAPTER 5

Maritime
Safety and Security

Like the Old West, a deserted inner-city street, or a burning apartment building, there is nothing more comforting than hearing and seeing someone who has come to rescue you from danger and possible death. At sea, the U.S. Coast Guard comes to the rescue.

Although the origin of the Coast Guard was not rooted in search and rescue or polar icebreaking, its has naturally evolved as events have driven its organization. The law of the sea is unbreakable and immutable—a life must be saved when it is in peril at sea. When the RMS *Titanic* foundered on April 15, 1912, after it struck an 800,000-ton iceberg, the United States helped lead the way to safer seas when the iceberg season began. When icebergs "calved" from their glaciers in Labrador, the USCG and the 17-nation International Ice Patrol tracked the bergs and notified mariners of their locations.

It was a short step from a small Revenue Marine Service (Revenue Cutter Service) to one of saving lives along the coastline (U.S. Life Saving Service), and from there to Search and Rescue (SAR). However, the small number of craft and vast territory to guard overwhelmed an already overworked group of men and women who staffed lifesaving stations and lighthouses. Surf boats, cutters, and anything from breeches buoy's to the infamous Lyle gun that could fire a rescue line hundreds of yards out to sea from

land during a howling storm was needed if men, women, and children were to be saved. Over a period of many years, funds and equipment finally began to trickle down to the working level. The total number of people saved from the origin of the USCG in 1915 to 2003 has been 162,413. These people would have perished at sea were it not for the men and women in blue who risk their lives and simply say, "Take my hand. I promise I will not let you go."

As cutters, surf boats, and aircraft have entered the inventory of the U.S. Coast Guard today, along with electronic detection capability, the art of saving lives at sea has become a science. The interior of a Jayhawk helicopter or a four-engine high-endurance HC-130 Hercules aircraft demonstrate the marriage of science and art in rescuing people at sea. However, no Coast Guard rescue swimmer has ever witnessed a machine or computer jump into freezing waters in a number five sea state to save a family clinging to the upturned hull of a capsized sailboat. It is still a part of the duty assigned to the rescue swimmer, and will likely remain so for the foreseeable future.

Search and Rescue (SAR)

What evolved from a small 10-cutter revenue-enforcement service that was on a par with the smallest nations in 1790 also pulled drowning people out of the water. A heritage

The old former Coast Guard cutter *Tamaroa* sits in the backwaters of Baltimore Harbor. It was the centerpiece of a rescue publicized in *The Perfect Storm* novel and movie. The vessel was the former USS *Zuni*, an old World War II U.S. Navy tug. *Author's Collection*

was developing, and no organizational changes or lack of funds could stop saving lives at sea. Search and rescue (SAR) has become one of the most visible of all U.S. Coast Guard activities. Interestingly, the process commands a mere 11 percent of the budget for this agency, although there is an additional 7 percent for Marine Safety in the 2004 budget that could be loosely interpreted as being part of SAR.

Bean counting aside, it is that rope being thrown, the Jayhawk overhead, or the rescue swimmer that means the most to someone who is going down for the third time. This is where the Coast Guard's reputation shines with the American public.

SAR became a formal fixture in the Coast Guard under Secretary of the Treasury in 1831, when he instructed the cutter *Gallatin* to sail up and down the East Coast of the United States with the specific mission to save lives at sea.

The word had spread throughout Western Europe that the new country to the west was

The USCG cutter *Tamaroa* attempts to save lives during a storm on October 31, 2000. *USCG*

open for settlement and that the feudal system was not in place or even recognized. People with sufficient funds booked passage on any type of sail or steam packet headed for the United States and a new beginning. Of course, the trip would be difficult, and landing on the New York, New Jersey, or Carolina shores during the storm seasons (October through April) was frequently perilous. There are few records of losses at sea during the early to middle 1800s, but thousands perished just yards from their goal.

Without Congressional approval, Treasury Secretary McLane employed the Revenue Marine cutters under his command and suspended some of their normal duties to aid mariners and shipwreck victims during the winter months on the East Coast. In 1837, this program was considered to be beneficial, and Congress authorized the President to delegate

This is a small Coast Guard Auxiliary craft at Ilwaco, Washington. The USCG performs a lot of boating-safety service for the Coast Guard and the public in terms of boating safety. *Author's Collection*

other craft to cruise coastal waters during severe-weather months to rescue mariners and shipwreck survivors.

Early lifesaving methods were crude. Shore stations included a Revenue Marine officer, a local board of underwriters to determine ship and cargo loss value, and citizens experienced in salvage and surf work. A boat, a wagon and horses, a breeches buoy, a Lyle gun for firing rope to a vessel impaled on rocks or grounded beyond the surf line, and plenty of whiskey were provided for the rescued and the rescuers.

The Civil War brought a stop to organized federal lifesaving, and reversed some of the progress that had been made. The Union Navy confiscated many of the lifesaving boats, and those that weren't used by the naval forces were used as slop carriers to feed hogs. When the war ended, the U.S. Life Saving Service, under Sumner L. Kimball, breathed life back into this vital service. From 1870 until 1915 when the Life Saving Service was merged with the Revenue Cutter Service to form the U.S. Coast Guard, the number of people saved along the coasts soared to nearly a 100 percent rescue rate. The coasts were all under the protection of the lifesaving stations, and thousands of immigrants owed their lives and property to the men and women of these stations. The core ideal under which the surf men operated was simple: You have to go out, but there is nothing in the book about you coming back. It still holds true for the men and women in the Coast Guard today.

One of the most famous lifesavers of the nineteenth century was Joshua James. He worked for the Massachusetts Humane Society as a Life Saving Station keeper. He first achieved fame when he and his surf men rescued many people from sinking schooners and other vessels that were breaking loose from their moorings during the great storm of 1888. Without fear for his own life, he went out many times to bring in stranded mariners. In the years that followed, he replicated his acts of bravery in snowstorms, ice storms, and monstrous gales. By the time he was 70, James was still ready and willing to pull out a wreck. For his courage in the face of an unforgiving sea and elements, he was awarded the Congressional and Massachusetts Life Saving medals. He was not alone in his devotion to saving others. Scores of men and women received little or no recognition for their efforts, but they sacrificed much to save others and help form the foundation of the modern U.S. Coast Guard.

This pour piper flush-deck destroyer was one of 20 older USN vessels used to enforce prohibition laws. The CG-17 was the former USS *Herndon* and was rammed and almost sunk in the fog by a cargo vessel. *Author's Collection*

Early Types of Lifesaving Equipment
Lifesaving in the early days involved wading into the surf and dragging people to safety. Warmth, food, and a generous dose of alcohol often revived the bedraggled survivors. Brush fires were frequently lit on bluffs at night during storms to signal ships to avoid rocks before ATON came into being. There was a shortage of small craft that could brave the surf to rescue the vessels that ran aground on unmarked rocks and shoals.

A boatload of marijuana was captured by intrepid Coasties on a river leading to Sacramento, California. The men, assigned to the Rio Vista station, seized dozens of marijuana plants in 2002. *USCG*

The first technique was to throw a rope attached to a floating object to mariners who attempted to reach the shore. This was effective, but only to a certain degree. The distance that a line could be thrown—normally a few yards—was based on a man's strength.

Experiments with explosive charges in a number of countries showed promise in offering more efficient lifesaving tools. Mortar, developed by English Army Captain George Manby, proved successful in 1808 when he first fired a line to stranded passengers and crew on the quickly sinking *Elizabeth* on the English coast. The mortar fired a line several hundred yards to the endangered people, and all were rescued. The mortar became a standard piece of lifesaving equipment for years.

Rockets as a line-throwing device were also developed from 1870 through 1910 and were responsible for saving an estimated 10,000 lives in England. However, the Hunt gun, developed by Edward Hunt in Massachusetts, eclipsed the

RIGHT: Three Stingray helicopters are all armed for combat against drug dealers or terrorists. *USCG*

The drug running *Sin Rumbo* is being pummeled by shellfire from the U.S. Navy destroyer USS *McCampbell* (DDG-85) on May 12, 2003. The USCG LEDET arrested the smugglers and confiscated over $20 million in high-grade cocaine from this sailboat. A few minutes later, the vessel was blown sky high by a five-inch shell. *U.S. Navy*

rocket. The key was to accurately throw a line a great distance. The rocket did not have the accuracy of an aimed gun.

Although Hunt's line-throwing device was highly acclaimed, the Lyle gun became the standard for the U.S. Life Saving Service. The Lyle gun was forged of bronze and weighed 185 pounds. It was invented by Captain David A. Lyle, a graduate of the military academy at West Point. Lyle was assigned to the west coast of the United States after the end of the Civil War. In 1877, he began to work closely with Sumner Kimball and Revenue Marine Captain James A. Merryman. Kimball was under pressure to develop an improved line-throwing device, and Lyle was assigned to work with the Life Saving Service to assist in this project. Lyle and others in the Life Saving Service experimented

There was $20 million of cocaine taken from the *Sin Rumbo*. *U.S. Navy*

with a small gun attached to a solid wooden carriage. Their work began in Springfield, Massachusetts, but the local populace was scared as projectiles and ropes flew about in all directions. The town's leaders, while sympathetic to the Life Saving Service, politely requested that they take their artillery to another location. Lyle and company quietly moved to Sandy Hook, New Jersey, and fired away for months. In 1878, a year after

beginning the project, the gun was perfected. A polished bronze barrel in a stout, yet small, wooden carriage was able to fire a 17-pound projectile, 14 inches in length, with an eye-bolt screwed into it. The record distance was 700 yards under optimum conditions. In real-life rescues, the throwing range was much less, but generally sufficient. Normally, the gun could be quickly transported to a wreck and within minutes fire a line (rather precisely) to willing hands that could secure a lifeline from shore to the wreck. Other devices that could do a similar or better job, but the Lyle gun was cheaper to build, easier to use and set up, and was accurate. The Lyle gun was used until 1962.

The breeches buoy, bosun's chairs, and lifecars were methods to help bring in wayward mariners and stranded passengers. First, a line had to be attached to the wreck, and then the buoy, lifecar, or bosun's chair was sent out to the wreck. The idea was simple. The people on the wreck would board the device and be pulled to shore. Of all the devices, the breeches buoy, which was a life ring with canvas attached to the bottom and holes for the person's legs, was considered the most successful. Even if the line broke or was lowered too far into the surf, the person had a chance of survival with the cork-filled life ring.

A number of other methods were developed to save lives, including boats that could endure the surf and wave action of a gale or storm, but a light was always needed. For this, the Coston signal was developed. It was a flare inserted into a brass holder attached to a wooden pike half the size of a marlin spike. The flares were bright and plentiful, and because many wrecks seemed to occur at night, the Coston signal was an invaluable tool.

The Life Saving Service soldiered on into the twentieth century and proved to be one of the taxpayers' best investments. Over 150,000 lives were saved by the men and women who served in the 189 stations nationwide. Ultimately, the service employed the 36-foot wooden motor lifeboats that enabled them to work miracles at sea. In 1913, the personnel in the U.S. Life Saving Service became aware that their days of independence were numbered and the fine Victorian architecture of the lifesaving stations and lighthouses would also fall under the axe. In 1915, the U.S. Life Saving Service and Revenue Cutter Service merged to create the U.S. Coast Guard.

Modern Methods

In the twentieth century, fixed- and rotary-wing aircraft became available to help search for mariners in distress. Surf boats, such as the famous 44-foot rollover craft and the new aluminum 47-foot surf boat, can quickly get to small craft in distress in almost any type of weather. However, to pull people to safety, a rigid-hull inflatable craft is necessary to get near rocky areas where the surf and waves swirl.

The search, rescue, and treatment of potentially injured boaters, hikers, and swimmers are not things that can be learned in a few days. It takes practice on a real-life stage. The Life Saving School in Ilwaco, Washington, is the perfect training ground for men and women to become surf rescue experts. The chief warrant officer, who is in command of the school, watches the Columbia River bar area with great interest to see if the waves and swells are high enough for his array of boats to roll over so his crews can be pushed to their limits, as in real-life rescue operations. Without this type of practice, including the employment of helicopters from the air rescue base across the river in Astoria, Oregon, the trainees would not be able to save lives. The intrepid surf men who lived at lifesaving stations along the coastlines have been replaced by a mix of surf craft, fixed- and rotary-wing aircraft, and electronic location devices.

The medium-endurance cutter *Legare* (MMEC-912) returns after it saved 201 Haitians who attempted to sail to the United States in November 2001. *USCG*

The RESCUE 21 program offers great promise for the future of lifesaving. The Coast Guard has taken a great leap of faith by earmarking $641 million of its limited resources to the program. Fundamentally, this program is designed to save lives through better and more-immediate communication.

RESCUE 21 seeks to eliminate the huge range of obsolete VHF-FM radio equipment at 270 Coast Guard facilities, over 700 remote transceiver sites around the nation, 700 Coast Guard vessels, and 3,000 portable radios. It is a daunting task, but when implemented, the program will make a quantum leap forward and

Flamingo Key is a waterless, foodless deserted island where 300 migrants were stranded after their boat foundered. The Coast Guard and Bahamian Navy brought food and water to the migrants, and after they received medical attention, they were returned to their homelands. Many had perished due to exposure and dehydration by the time help arrived. *USCG*

will allow communication between those in distress and the Coast Guard. It will enable the Coast Guard to pinpoint the origin of contact within two degrees and will improve the chance to save mariners that have called for assistance.

Illegal Drug Interdiction

To most, the United States began to prevent illegal drugs from entering the country in the 1970s. The first actual seizure occurred on August 31, 1890, when the Revenue cutter, USRC *Wolcott,* stopped the SS *George E. Starr* as the U.S.-flagged steamer made its way through the Straits of Juan de Fuca into Washington State. On a routine search for contraband and illegal immigrants, the boarding crew discovered a large amount of opium that had not been declared for customs payment. At that time, opium was legal in the United States for medicinal purposes, but it was very addictive and subject to abuse.

So began the Quiet War, which has raged at sea, on land, and in the air for over 113 years. The United States has not been the only nation to fight drug smugglers, and as the stakes become ever higher, the methods become even more drastic. Few nations go to such great lengths as the United States to protect the rights and lives of smugglers and guarantee due process. Five to 50 years in prison is the usual punishment for possession, and smugglers who sell commercially or attempt to transport drugs across some national borders simply disappear without benefit of trial or notification of their whereabouts.

As with all wars, each side must outdo the other in order to win, and the stakes, which run into billions of dollars per year, give the smugglers an edge. They can pay off local officials and purchase aircraft and speedboats to smuggle drugs. The sheer amount of money involved can cause drug runners to take chances by fighting back with heavier weaponry, including shoulder-launched surface-to-air or surface-to-surface missiles, low-radar-signature surface craft, and diesel submarines. The going price for a working *Foxtrot*-class diesel submarine with a 12,000 nautical mile range, diving depth of over 500 feet, and a top speed of 19 knots surfaced is $50,000. These craft, along with several other types of older Soviet bloc boats, dot the globe as museum ships or sit in backwaters. About 200 craft are available in varying condition, but they are quiet and can carry a large tonnage of drugs, along with a torpedo complement that may still be operational. As illegal drug prices increase and profits soar, drug cartels may explore this possibility, and the Coast Guard might again find itself fighting U-boats, albeit stateless.

The USCG and Prohibition

Before fighting illegal drugs, the Coast Guard fought the Rum Wars, which were the result of the 18th Amendment to the Constitution, also called the National Prohibition (Volstead) Act. The amendment prohibited the manufacture, sale, import, export, and consumption of alcoholic beverages on American soil effective January 16, 1920.

The public and government were lulled into a sense of false security by the simplicity of the act. After all, who could stand up and state that they supported drunkenness in public, crime, murder, and all of the evils that alcohol always brought. Of course, piety in church on Sunday morning was far different from hangin' one on with your fellows after a hard day's work. The prohibitionists and axe-wielding, rum-barrel smashers really misjudged the pulse of the national heartbeat this time. Unfortunately, January 17, 1920, dawned, and one Washington agency after another tried to shuffle the responsibility somewhere else, and it ended up at the gangplank of the U.S. Coast Guard. Of course, much of the illegal liquor in the United States was made in bathtubs and backwoods stills. Unfortunately, many of the local sheriffs, marshals, constables, and police were somewhere in the economic chain that made up the local illegal liquor trade. Scotch whiskey was often made from 180-proof alcohol, brown food coloring, and a teaspoon of iodine.

There were millions of dollars to be made,

and soon there were entrepreneurs in this business at one level or another. For those elected to get the real stuff, the liquor had to come via the sea or across the Mexican or Canadian borders. Much of it came over the sea, and the Coast Guard that had to watch every possible cove, inlet, and waterway leading into the United States.

At first, the Coast Guard's cutters did not stand a chance against the rummies, and the ships hovering beyond the 12-mile safety limit were protected by law from interception. The Coast Guard had a few cutters and even fewer craft for inshore work. A smattering of subchasers were loaned by the Navy, but their speed barely topped 20 knots. New craft were built as funds became available. The rummies' profits were rumored to be over 700 percent per run, and their opposition was paid $21 per month. The picture was bleak until the U.S. Navy offered to loan more ships to fight the smugglers.

Ultimately, the USCG acquired 29 destroyers from the U.S. Navy that ranged from the early lightly armed flivvers that traveled at 32 knots, to flush deckers that could reach a top speed of 35 knots. Since scores of destroyers were laid up after World War I, the U.S. Navy also loaned 11 1,000-tonners that were slightly less capable at 29 knots. The USCG made good use of them and was able to chase down and seize or destroy the rummies with these higher-speed, well armed ships. Prohibition ended on December 5, 1933. At best, it was estimated that the USCG prevented a mere five percent of illegal alcohol from entering the United States. The Coast Guard struggled desperately to win, but the odds were too high.

A Stateless, but Dangerous War

Since the beginning of the 1960s, the flow of illegal drugs from East Asia, the Near East, and Central and South America has been an openly incurable plague on the United States and other Western nations.

Simplistic suggestions ranging from former First Lady Nancy Reagan's "Just Say No" program to complex solutions involving precision weapons, electronics, and a large portion of the U.S. military and Coast Guard have been employed to stop or slow down the flow of drugs. The Coast Guard has finally settled upon a goal to reduce the overall influx of illegal drugs—primarily cocaine and marijuana—by under 20 percent. The U.S. government recognizes that although there is zero tolerance, there is also zero chance of reaching this objective given the resources available.

Unfortunately, the same story has been replayed over and over for years with illegal drugs entering the United States. However, this may change as the USCG and Navy team up to fight this scourge. The Navy has been actively involved with ships, such as the former nuclear cruiser USS *California* (CGN-36), and a number of frigates including the USS *McInerney* (FFG-8) based out of Mayport, Florida. Most of the Navy and Coast Guard vessels used to search for drug runners carry helicopters. The Coast Guard employs its *Famous*- and *Reliance*-class cutters for much of the anti-drug activity. The *Famous*-class cutters are 1,820 tons full load at 270 feet in length and carry a main battery of a 76mm gun, .50-caliber machine guns, and two SRBOC launchers. The *Famous* class, which is capable of 19.5 knots,

The *Mackinaw,* the oldest icebreaker in the Coast Guard inventory, has since been painted red to stand out against the ice. The *Mackinaw* will be replaced by a modern vessel by with the same name. *USCG*

carries one of three different types of helicopters. The *Reliance* class is 210 feet in length with a 1,020-ton full-load displacement and is capable of 18 knots. They are armed with a single 25mm Bushmaster gun and .50-caliber weapons. *Reliance*-class ships also have facilities for one of two types of helicopters. This gives them over-the-horizon surveillance and attack capability. This is something that the go-fast drug runner boats will encounter. A go-fast boat is a high-speed craft with two huge outboard engines and enough fuel to take them from loading areas in South America to North America at speeds over 40 knots. On board these craft are two or three drug smugglers, illegal drugs worth

These small inland waterway tug/icebreakers keep waterways open for local traffic. The *Katmai Bay* (WTGB-101) is based in Sault Ste. Marie, Michigan, and the *Biscayne Bay* (WTGB-104) is based in St. Ignace, Michigan. *USCG*

millions of dollars, and gasoline. The drug cartels are now exploring the use of stealth technology to improve the chances of high-speed craft getting through the Coast Guard's "steel web."

The Coast Guard employs its *Island* class for inshore patrol activity. These rugged 110-foot craft are highly capable and can travel up to 29.5 knots. They carry a 25mm Bushmaster gun and .50-caliber machine guns or 12.7mm machine guns, depending on the craft.

The go-fast boats are just one threat to the Coast Guard. There are many others, including small freighters and expensive and innocuous-looking sailboats. Not long ago, Colombian police discovered a small submarine under construction to transport drugs northward, so the threat could eventually come from under the sea.

Today, the illegal-drug war seems to be restricted to surface craft. The vessels used by drug cartels are acquired from a number of sources, and many are illegal. Some of the pleasure craft have been stolen at sea by pirates and the craft are sufficiently modified to conceal their original identity.

The Coast Guard and Navy Work Together to Fight Drugs

The *Arleigh Burke*-class USS *McCampbell* (DDG-85) and her sisters of the Flight IIA variant have improved electronics and rotary-wing capability. Originally, 51 *Arleigh Burke*-class destroyers were to be built, but the Navy has proposed to increase that number to 61, with the final vessels joining the fleet in 2010. Now, the Navy is exploring an entire family of smaller land-attack vessels or littoral combat ships (LCS).

In terms of guns, there are a number of places along the rails of the ship for smaller-caliber weapons (shielded .50-caliber machine guns) to defend the ship. The forward-mounted Mark 45 5-inch, .62-caliber, single-barrel guns that can fire standard 13.5-mile-range munitions and the new extended-range guided munitions (ERGM), which have a range of 63 nautical miles, are very impressive. The *McCampbell* carries up to 232 rounds of this ammunition.

What makes this vessel a Flight IIA is its aviation unit. There are two permanent hangers aft with a landing deck on the fantail. The ship carries two SH-60B/R Seahawks, which can land with help from the recovery, assist, secure and traverse (RAST) system. When the helos are not in use, they are stored in their respective hangars with their rotors folded inward. The helos are capable of carrying a Mark 46 or Mark 50 ASW torpedo, Penguin and Hellfire antiship missiles, 25 active or passive sonobuoys, and the APS-124 airborne radar system.

When the *McCampbell* was on its first deployment on an illegal-drug suppression patrol, it was assigned the *Battlecats* of the helicopter antisubmarine squadron light (HSL) 43 Detachment 5. These helos and their crews played a crucial role in a confrontation on May 12, 2003.

Destroyer Versus Drug Runner

In the early hours of May 12, 2003, off the Central American coast, the USS *McCampbell* detected a pleasure craft named *Sin Rumbo* with Canadian registration. The *Sin Rumbo*, a 52-foot, single-masted sailing craft was asked to heave to for inspection. At the same time, a helo was launched to observe and provide protection from the air. The U.S. Coast Guard LEDET boarded the craft quietly and began a search. The team discovered 1.36 metric tons of high-grade cocaine wrapped in waterproof cartons worth an estimated $20 million. The crew of the *Sin Rumbo* had little or no explanation for the contraband.

The smugglers were arrested and taken back to the *McCampbell*, as was the cocaine via the ships RIB. Then, the captain gave the order to

The RMS *Titanic* struck an iceberg on April 14, 1912, and sank the following morning at 1:40 A.M. Many rules and regulations have changed as the result of this horrendous loss. *Ulster Transport Museum*

blow the *Sin Rumbo* out of the water with the 5-inch, .62-caliber weapons. The sailing craft exploded and disappeared after a few rounds, and the *McCampbell* chalked one up for itself and its crew. It was the embodiment of cooperation between the Coast Guard and the Navy.

The Coast Guard routinely fights in the Quiet War. The frigate USS *McInerney* (FFG-8) seized 11,000 pounds of cocaine when it intercepted a go-fast boat off Panama. Since October 1, 2002, the Coast Guard has seized 67,000 pounds of cocaine and 9,000 pounds of marijuana.

The battles continue and often take place with less spectacular results, but every victory, large or small, hurts the drug trade. In March 2003, 2,778 pounds of cocaine was seized 240 miles south of Acapulco, Mexico, by a LEDET from the high-endurance cutter *Munro*. Three smugglers were detained.

The Jacksonville, Florida, Coast Guard Unit played a major role in the capture of over 138,000 pounds of high-grade cocaine and 283 smugglers in 2003. HITRON aircraft were instrumental in these successes. The cutter *Tampa* recovered 4,494 pounds of cocaine and captured five smugglers with its MH-68A Stingray helo south of Jamaica in late 2003.

Other nations feel the affect of drug sales and trade. The USCG works with Columbia to help counter the Revolutionary Armed Forces of Columbia, the Army of National Liberation, and the United Self Defense Forces. In Northern Ireland, drug money funds activities of the Irish Republican Army, which has advisors who assist South and Central American revolutionary groups. Peru has been struck by the Shining Path, and Mexico still faces the Zapatista National Liberation Army.

The production, sale, and use of illegal narcotics is a growing and dangerous threat to the world that spreads quickly with addiction and easy access of money. The USCG, DEA, Marine Corps, and other goverments are doing what they can with their limited resources, but the victory still remains beyond their grasp.

Other Forms of Contraband

There is a tendency to focus on illegal drugs as the contraband of choice when referring to the U.S. Coast Guard and the Customs Service, but there are other types of contraband. These items, generally intercepted at points of entry to the U.S., are more diverse, but of less interest to most citizens. Absinthe or derivatives of *artemisia absinthium* are some of the most potent and addictive drugs known to man. Ceramic tableware must be examined to determine the presence of unacceptably high levels of lead, which can cause lead poisoning and other health problems.

Cultural artifacts from Asia have become a hot commodity that smugglers attempt to sneak into the United States, as well as products made from cat and dog fur, which were finally outlawed in 2000. Trophy skins, animal heads, and other artifacts of rare and endangered animals are also forbidden.

Any items that would enrich the regimes of the Taliban, Iraq, Iran, Libya, Serbia, Cuba, and the Sudan, such as gold and silver coins are forbidden. Diet drugs and narcotics not approved by the Food and Drug Administration are also forbidden. Those who attempt to break or circumvent the law are usually arrested, typically receive stiff fines, and have their passports noted.

Illegal Migrant Interdiction

It is estimated that the Coast Guard has interdicted more than 305,000 illegal migrants from 62 countries since 1980. The flood of undocumented aliens comes mainly from China, Cuba, the Dominican Republic, and Haiti. They come to the United States to seek a better life with a job, home, food, and education for their children. It is difficult to blame someone for wanting such a future, but by illegally entering the United States, they have broken federal law and subject themselves to a life of running from the law.

Since the 1979 Mariel Boatlift, the Coast Guard has stepped up its efforts to prevent illegal aliens or migrants from entering the United States via the sea. In 1999, 1,092 people attempted to come ashore from China; 37,678 were turned back from Haiti in 1992; 38,560 from Cuba were turned away in 1994; and 6,273 were sent home to the Dominican Republic in 1996. Sometimes the craft that migrants attempted to travel in fell apart, but the numbers were never recorded because these people were consumed by the sea. The Coast Guard has had to deal with so many illegal aliens that they have created several different migrant interdiction efforts: Operation Able Manner/Uphold Democracy for Haitians, Operation Able Vigil for Cubans, and Operation Able Response for Dominicans.

People attempting to make their way to the United States have been attacked by sharks, and then by land sharks after arrival because so many people take advantage of their vulnerability. Drug smugglers have mixed in with migrant groups and carried drugs to the United States under the guise of being illegal migrants.

They knew that they would have to stay in the United States for a short period of time before being sent back to their homeland.

Polar Icebreaking and International Ice Patrol

The northern regions of the United States, such as Alaskan waters and the Great Lakes, freeze over during winter, but commerce must continue. This is where the Coast Guard deploys its aging fleet of powerful icebreakers to punch out ice-free lanes for ships to pass. Breakers also free vessels caught in the ice and rescue crews that are ice bound.

The Coast Guard has a number of icebreakers that range from the larger version *Polar Star, Polar Sea*, and *Mackinaw* to the smaller harbor icebreakers that break up ice as thick as six feet. Smaller harbor icebreakers can only push aside flow ice, but the larger icebreakers can thrust their heavy steel reinforced bows up on the ice and smash it into smaller pieces. It is a slow and tedious process, but commerce must continue.

Two of the major icebreakers, the *Polar Sea* and *Polar Star,* work in the far northern reaches of the world to ensure that supply vessels can get through to scientific expeditions and military operations.

New icebreakers are planned for the Coast Guard, beginning with the replacement 240-foot *Mackinaw* that will replace the World War II-built *Mackinaw* that served the Great Lakes since 1944. The new icebreaker will begin service in October 2005. The rationale behind the Coast Guard's responsibility for icebreaking is contained in federal laws that date back to 1936. Of course, icebreaking and protection of vessels from ice has not been restricted to inland waters.

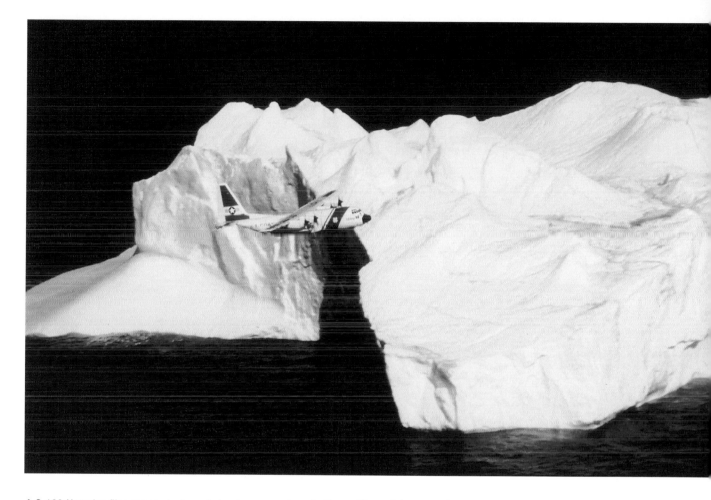

A C-130 Hercules flies over an iceberg during ice season to radio the positions of dangerous bergs and ice flows to the International Ice Patrol headquarters. This enables mariners to avoid collisions. *USCG*

The initial efforts of the International Ice Patrol were crude and slow, but with the full advent of radio communications, aircraft with greater range, and vessels that could patrol the area during ice season, the patrol could warn mariners of the dangers of ice flows and bergs. The U.S. Coast Guard attempted to destroy some of the larger bergs with gunfire and explosives, but these were ineffective. Carbon dust was spread on the bergs to enhance melting, but that also failed, so common sense took over and ship owners routinely check for the location of bergs that are plotted by the patrol. Avoidance is the best way to remain

The USCG *Bayberry*, a cargo boom vessel and tug, has pushed a barge into place to extend its apparatus to dragging in an oil spill. These vessels are rare, but essential when oil pollution strikes a beautiful coastline. The *Bayberry* works with barge No. 60044, which is designed for trapping oil spills. *USCG*

afloat! The patrol often consists of C-130 Hercules aircraft that patrol "iceberg alley" daily during iceberg season (February to July), and radio the headquarters of the International Ice Patrol in Groton, Connecticut, to advise all ships of berg activity.

Avoiding bergs is one thing, but with an immovable $5 billion offshore oil rig like the Hibernia, it is imperative that bergs do not drift into the drilling platform and disturb pumping operations. The M/V *Norseman*, a 2,600-ton vessel, is crewed with personnel skilled in "catching and towing" icebergs. The average large berg (250,000 tons or more) travels southward at approximately one knot per hour. The *Norseman* and her sister ship, the M/V *Nascopie,* wrangle errant bergs by placing ropes around them and towing them out of the path of the oil rig.

Natural Resource Protection

The Coast Guard began its role as a protector of natural resources nearly 100 years before it was formally created. The Revenue Marine was ordered to protect the U.S. Government's stock of Florida live oaks. The British Navy had marked thousands of trees in the northern regions of the new country as prime lumber for ship building. The Revenue Marine told the British Navy it was not possible to reap this harvest. It seemed as if poachers looking for good timber continuously visited the shores of the new nation with the intent to cut down the finest woods to sell in Europe. By 1822, laws had been passed that put teeth into the Revenue Marine's seizure of contraband and levied stiff fines and prison sentences for those caught.

Aside from timber, the Revenue Marine, and then the Coast Guard, were given the task to prevent the killing of seals, whales, and all fur-bearing animals. Fishing trawlers moved into Alaskan waters, the Bering Sea, and off the East and West Coasts and harvested everything that could swim. Sea turtles, dolphins, small whales, salmon, cod, and every type of fish was indiscriminately hauled up into the bowels of the giant ships owned by Soviet and Japanese syndicates.

The fish were slaughtered and the offal was thrown overboard. When American fishermen, who were subject to fish and game laws, attempted to make a living, few fish were left after the huge harvests made by giant foreign interests. More than 110,000 commercial fishing boats legally operate from U.S. ports and compete for every last legal-sized fish. The fishing grounds must be managed because the industry produces $25 billion in annual revenue. In the early 1990s, almost five million metric tons of fish were being harvested each year. To maintain this output, the Coast Guard will have to take an even-greater stand against poachers and illegal fishing combines that do not obey the rules for fish resource management.

Natural resource protection also means preventing waterways from becoming polluted with oil, garbage, chemicals, and other contaminants. Substances such as whiskey or alcohol dumped in a river will kill thousands of sea creatures. But the worst is crude oil. When oil vessels run aground or collide, they dump their bulk oil cargo and their own fuel bunkerage into the water, killing countless birds, animals, and fish that depend on the sea.

No one will ever forget the huge oil spill that covered Prince William Sound in 1989 when the oil tanker *Exxon Valdez* ran aground and its cargo of crude oil flowed out to contaminate the entire area. This was not the first ecological nightmare, nor will it be the last. Steps have been taken to lessen the impact of vessels carrying huge cargoes of oil that might run aground or collide with other vessels. Specially designed oil response ships and crews are stationed up and down U.S. coasts and are available 24/7 to help contain oil spills. The Coast Guard also has a strike force with equipment to contain and clean up oil spills anywhere in the world. One of their sterling successes was the cleanup of diesel fuel from the tanker *Jessica* in the Galápagos Islands. The inter-island tanker grounded on January 16, 2001. With the help of the Coast Guard pollution strike force, volunteers, and the Venezuelan government, the spill was contained and very little damage was done.

Another oil spill occurred in Buzzards Bay on April 27, 2003 that threatened the coastal area of Massachusetts. Bouchard Transportation's Barge No. 120 grounded and its number two starboard tank ruptured. Nearly 15,000 gallons of oil flowed into the bay. This particular area is the home of the tern, a seabird, and its breeding ground, so immediate action was necessary. By April 29, 2003, a barge was alongside the stricken No. 120 and pumped out the remaining oil. Unfortunately, the strike force couldn't save all of the wildlife, but its quick action did prevent a massive catastrophe.

Until recently, many vessels discharged garbage and other waste directly into the sea. This was sometimes done while a ship was in harbor. Today, ships that come to and from American ports must utilize holding tanks to carry waste water and store garbage until it can be properly disposed ashore. As an example, cruise ships that enter American ports connect to holding tank pumps, and garbage trucks haul away all other waste for land disposal. Any ship dumping in a U.S. harbor is subject to stiff fines. With the forensic methods now available, the Coast Guard can easily find the vessels that violate these laws.

The Coast Guard and state and federal environmental protection agencies have made significant progress since the days when 10 or 20 vessels dumped waste water and garbage at sea or in harbors in the dark of night.

Foreign Vessel Inspection

Ships that enter U.S. ports are examined and inspected by specialized boarding teams from the U.S. Coast Guard. The Drug Enforcement Agency occasionally inspects ships in search of contraband and illegal migrants.

In addition to determining the seaworthiness of a vessel entering a U.S. port, under the new homeland security mandates, ships also must be inspected for the possibility of terrorism. Container ships are coming under increased scrutiny because the hundreds of metal containers make ideal hiding places for weapons, contraband, and people. Until recently, a mere two percent of the containers was examined. The results of the increased inspections are promising.

Vessels entering U.S. ports are also examined to determine if they can maneuver in the available waters and if their draft is too great for the allotted mooring area. These things, including searching for oil leaks, are what a boarding team must look into before a ship is allowed to settle into a U.S. harbor.

Occasionally vessels will steam toward U.S. coastlines, ram themselves into the surf, and allow hundreds of illegal aliens to scatter into the brush and countryside. This has occurred in the San Francisco area with illegal Chinese immigrants. The Coast Guard tracks the vessels far out to sea and has successfully reduced the incidence of these occurrences. Foreign vessel inspection can take a more exotic turn when the ship is one of the newer cruise liners that

The Greek *Helleport Alhambra* is the largest vessel to enter U.S. waters. It carries 400,000 gallons of crude oil in its double hull. Despite every precaution, it will be examined by the Los Angeles Marine Safety Office of the USCG. The ship is 1,300 feet in length, which is 200 feet longer than a 90,000-ton *Nimitz*-class aircraft carrier. *USCG*

has problems with massive illness or has illegally dumped its tanks. Specially trained dogs are used to sniff out narcotics.

To sum up, foreign vessel inspection can range from searching for illegal drugs to verifying the correct licenses of all officers to ensuring that the vessel will not cause any harm or disruption to the harbor or port. It is a massive undertaking, especially with the new homeland security mandates.

The U.S. Navy *Cyclone*-class patrol coastal boats were magnificent very useful additions in the war in Iraq. They could get in close where destroyers and cruisers couldn't. They worked well in concert with the USCG. Here, the *Firebolt* (PC-10) sits at Camp Patriot in Kuwait and is ready to work with Coast Guard personnel and the 110-foot *Island*-class and Raider boats. *U.S. Navy*

 Integrated Deepwater Project and the Future

For seagoing SAR or drug-interdiction patrols, the Coast Guard has a mixture of high- and medium-endurance cutters and a number of other craft that perform harbor patrol, tend to buoys, and keep ports free of ice in the Great Lakes and Alaska. Their motto is that they can turn a dime into a quarter and know how use their resources to the best effect. Much of the equipment, aircraft, and boats are out of date, and the Coast Guard needs money to improve its ability to meet all of its commitments. This is the purpose of the Integrated Deepwater Project.

In essence, the Integrated Deepwater Project is a fully integrated and modernized upgrade of the U.S. Coast Guard that uses a systems approach to the functions and missions of the Coast Guard. For years, the Coast Guard has had to make do with whatever it could squeeze out of the government. Despite the obvious need for a Coast Guard and the desperate need the nation has for a maritime guardian, funds have not been forthcoming as they have for the military services in the Department of Defense.

The Deepwater System will upgrade some of the modern units, discard older systems, and add items such as HAE-UAV unmanned air vehicles. This unmanned air vehicle can provide surveillance for up to 38 hours at a range of 12,500 nautical miles, send real-time images back to a cutter or shore station, and save crew time. The AB-139 VRS helicopters will be carried by almost all helo-capable cutters, and surface-ship improvements will include the national security cutter (NSC), which is 421 feet in length and carries helos, unmanned vehicles, and a crew of 82 with an endurance of 60 days and a range of 12,000 miles. The European twin-engine CASA EADS Maritime Patrol aircraft will replace the aging fleet of C-130 Hercules. The CASA EADS aircraft have a range of 3,055 nautical miles, state-of-the-art avionics, removable electronic and weapons packages dependent on selected missions, and are fully integrated with all other surface ship and unmanned flight assets. The CASA 235 will effectively search out targets, whether illegal-drug craft or SAR candidates at long ranges.

The unmanned air vehicle with high-endurance capability will have a minimum 30-hour endurance and a range of 12,500 miles. Along with other unmanned systems, it will help save lives. The Coast Guard's surface ships will include 8 large national security cutters, 25 offshore patrol cutters, and an entire family of smaller craft to replace the aging fleet.

Homeland Security Mandates

Harbors and waterways all over the world are vulnerable to terrorist attacks. Most foreign ports do not have the defenses in place that are currently established under the U.S. Coast Guard and the Department of Homeland Security. The United States is making substantial progress to

The former Long Beach Naval shipyard is now a container ship depot operated by Mainland Chinese interests. The USCG protects this facility from harm. *Author's Collection*

improve the overall protection of its ports and waterways, but there is still much to be done.

There are at least 30 major ports and waterways that face the oceans surrounding our nation, including Guam, Hawaii, and Alaska, that require layered defense against terrorist threats. There are a like number that require strengthened protection. Unfortunately, most are easy targets, and with ingenuity, dedication, and funding, many could be sealed for weeks or months against seaborne traffic. This could interrupt foreign trade, prevent military shipping, and block oil and gas lines. In selected harbors, including Miami and Fort Lauderdale, Florida, and San Pedro, California, the cruise ship industry could be paralyzed. Shutting down Charleston, South Carolina; New Orleans, Louisiana; Long Beach, California; Oakland, California; and Seattle, Washington, would put a huge dent in our ability to maintain an import/export balance of trade. The ports of Long Beach, Seattle, and Charleston are expanding to handle more traffic from larger vessels that

remain in port just long enough to unload, reload, and depart. Richmond and Benicia, California, handle a growing number of imported automobiles from the Far East, and an interruption of this trade could have a negative impact on foundational trade.

Container distribution centers have been built on all of our coasts, and ships come and go like clockwork. Much of our trade comes via container or oil tankers from all parts of the world. Similarly, the United States exports goods and products along the same routes from the same harbors. The container business is so brisk that ships slated to carry empty containers find it more profitable to discard the containers and have new ones that will be filled with cargo awaiting shipment built at their destination. It seems odd that nearly new well-built steel containers should be sacrificed for rapid-profit-motivated turnaround time, but that is the nature of trade today. Most modern vessels now have thrusters aft and stern to "self dock" and remove the cost and time of tugboats. Sea trade is more valuable today than ever before, and a ship that remains without cargo is money lost in the highly competitive shipping world. Our harbors hold the key to our national economy, and although high-profile political targets grab headlines, low-profile targets can do the most damage if properly interrupted.

Most natural or manmade harbors are entered through channels or narrow arteries that lead to deep water anchorages, moorings, and piers. During the eighteenth, nineteenth and early twentieth centuries, a safe harbor kept storms at bay and allowed adequate harbor defense by military shore batteries. Ships and ports could be protected from enemy warships with relative ease, and harbors that had a natural deep channel were considered to be premium locations for trade centers. The airplane, with its ability to carry bombs, and a skillfully maneuvered submarine quickly countered the advantages of natural harbors. Many harbors were defended during World War II with submarine netting, but this proved more of a hindrance to access/egress than actual protection. Coast-defense guns became tourist museums or storage sites, but the United States continues to use the same harbors for its warships and commercial trade. After all, they are still the best anchorages available, and a considerable investment had been made in the infrastructure of local commercial trade.

Harbor improvement is not merely for commercial purposes. The military is building new piers and access points for its major fleet units. The U.S. Navy is building additional aircraft carrier facilities at North Island in San Diego Bay to accommodate the nuclear carriers USS *John Stennis* (CVN-74) and USS *Nimitz* (CVN-68). The USS *Ronald Reagan* (CVN-76) will replace the *Stennis,* which will move to Bremerton, Washington, in 2005 to replace the USS *Carl Vinson* (CVN-70). The *Vinson* is due for a refueling and complex overhaul (RCOH) in 2004. In any event, it is possible that 2 of our 12 carriers could be boxed up along with much of the Third Fleet in the San Diego Harbor if the entrance to the bay were blocked or closed. Considering that the *Eisenhower* (CVN-69) and *Stennis* will be undergoing RCOH and the *Constellation* is retired, that would leave the U.S. Navy with seven active carriers, the same number it had before the beginning of World War II.

This 25-foot Port Security Unit *Raider* craft was built by Boston Whaler. It is capable of 40 knots, is powered by two outboard engines, and carries a .50-caliber machine gun forward and two M-60 machine guns amidships. *USCG*

The U.S. Coast Guard, civilian police, and harbor patrols are doing their best to protect our harbors and waterways, but the effort is far from adequate and is taxing their resources beyond measure. The Coast Guard is stretched beyond capability, and years of cost-cutting and low budgets have finally caught up to our coast defense force. The announcement that four major bridges in California were suspected terrorist targets in November 2001 caused the Coast Guard to withdraw much of its harbor and coastal patrol vessels from other areas to guard these bridges. Nothing happened, and, in reality, the collapse or destruction of the Richmond Bridge, which was not on the probable target list, would have done more damage by preventing the flow of oil to Martinez and the manufacture of other vital petroleum products in that immediate area. Likewise, the blockage of the channel under the high expanse over the Columbia River in Astoria would have done far greater economic damage to the Pacific Northwest.

This Port Security Unit guarded the Khawr al Amaya oil terminal in Iraq and will return to the U.S. to perform the same task. *USCG*

A 41-foot utility boat escorts a huge cruise ship out of the harbor. The people aboard the cruise ship M/V *Star Princess* know that the U.S. Coast Guard has examined their ship for safety issues, and sea marshals have been present to seek out undesirable passengers. An armed craft escorts the giant ship out to sea. *USCG*

It is incorrect to think that the main role of the U.S. Coast Guard is to save the lives of unlucky mariners and capture illegal immigrants. The Coast Guard is the most appreciated yet underrated quasi-military/law enforcement force in the U.S. arsenal. Its motto: *Semper Paratus* (always ready) is stretched tight to meet its ever-increasing tasking. The primary missions of the U.S. Coast Guard are to:

- Provide safety and SAR at sea. The Coast Guard saved 3,700 lives and over $1 billion in property in 1999.
- Provide national defense. This includes maritime intercept, deployed port security, peacetime engagement of enemies, and environmental defense operations.

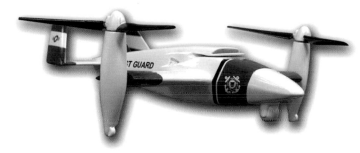

The maritime patrol aircraft (MPA) is produced by CASA-EADS and will be employed by many foreign governments. This aircraft will serve as an adjunct to the H-130 Hercules, which is scheduled for an upgrade. *USCG*

The vertical takeoff and landing (VTOL) unmanned vehicle (VUAV) is called and Eagle Eye and is produced by Bell as the HV-911. These aircraft will enable much more extensive coverage of larger ocean areas known as Ocean Domain Awareness. *USCG*

- Provide maritime security, including counter-terrorism and illegal-drug interdiction and suppression. There were 132,919 pounds of cocaine interdicted in 2000.
- Provide mobility such as maintenance of over 50,000 ATONs and lighthouses and ensure that shipping can traverse ice-clogged waterways.
- Protect natural resources, including endangered species, enforce fisheries acts, and contain oil or chemical spills.

For a seafaring nation that has thousands of miles of coastline and a well-defined series of inland waterways and major lakes, the number of Coast Guard aircraft and vessels is far too small to meet all of the nation's demands, especially when harbor-defense needs have dramatically increased. We need to protect our harbors and waterways at all times. This is vital to our survival as a nation. Building additional

ships, small craft, and aircraft will take time, but certain vessels from the U.S. Navy can be transferred to the Department of Homeland Defense to augment the Coast Guard and state and local patrol craft.

The Coast Guard's Role in the Twenty-first Century

Vessels thought to be useful only in time of war can be used for missions that were never considered high priority. The mere presence of harbor patrol craft can be sufficient to discourage overt terrorism and keep our sea lanes open for commerce and the movement of our Navy. The U.S. Navy and Coast Guard must continue to combine assets to protect our harbors and waterways. There will be new threats to freedom and the U.S. homeland, but in the end the Coast Guard will be always ready.

Bibliography

Ambrose, A. J., ed., *Jane's Merchant Review*, 1982, Jane's

Bonner & Bonner, *Warship Boneyards*, 2000, MBI

Bonnett, Wayne, *Build Ships*, 1999, Wingate Press

Bonsall, Thomas E., *Titanic,* 1987, Gallery Books

Cairis, Nicholas T., *Passenger Liners of the World Since 1893,* 1979, Bonanza Books

Call Bulletin newspaper files, 1994, Courtesy of Treasure Island Museum

Coast Guard for the 21st Century. 2003

Dunn, Laurence, *Liners and Their Recognition*, 1954, The Blackmore Press

Fort Bragg Advocate, June 27, 2003

Gibbs, Jim, *Peril at Sea*, 1986, Schiffer Publishing

Gibbs, Jim, *Shipwrecks of the Pacific Coast*, 1957, Binfort and Mort

Hudson, Kenneth & Nicholls, Ann, *Tragedy on the High Seas*, 1979, A & W Publishers

Integrated Deepwater System. 2003

Larkins, William T, *U.S. Navy Aircraft 1921-1941*, 1961, Aviation History Publications

Maddocks, Melvin, *The Great Liners*, 1978, Time Life Books

Marine News, Journal of the World Ship Society Date

McMillan, Beverly &Lehrer, Stanley, *Titanic—fortune and fate*, 1998, Simon and Schuster

Miller Jr., William H., *Great Cruise Ships* (Trilogy from 1897–1990), 1988, Dover Books

Morris, Douglas, *Cruisers of the Royal and Commonwealth Navies,* 1987, Maritime Books

Noble, William P., *The Perilous Sea,* 1985, Yankee Publishing

Perkes, Dan, *Eyewitness to Disaster*, 1976, Hammond Incorporated

Pitt, Barrie, *The Battle of the Atlantic*, 1980, Time-Life Books

Quinn, William P, *Shipwrecks Along the Atlantic Coast*, 1988, Parnassus Imprints

Robertson, Morgan, *The Wreck of the Titan or Futility*, 1898, M. F. Mansfield

Sea Breezes

Ed Schnepf, *Sea Classics.* Challenge Publications. 20th Century Fox/Paramount Pictures

Sea Power, Navy League of the United States. 1982

Shanks, Ralph, York, Wicks, Shanks, Lisa Woo, *The U.S. Life Saving Service,* 1196, Costano Books

Shield of Freedom IUSCG & USCG Reserve. 2003

Silverstone, Paul H., *U.S. Warships of World War II*, 1970, Doubleday

Stephens, Hugh W., *The Texas City Disaster 1947*, 1997, University of Texas Press

Stern, Steven B., *Stern's Guide to the Cruise Vacation, 2002*, 2002, Pelican Publishing

Sweetman, Jack, *American Naval History*, 1984, Naval Institute Press

U.S. Customs Regulations for U.S. Residents, 2003

Various, *The United States Coast Guard*, 2002, Government Services Group

Wheeler, Eugene & Kalian, Robert, *Shipwrecks and Smugglers,* 1984, Pathfinder Publishing

Williams, David, *Wartime Disasters at Sea*, 1997, Patrick Stephens Limited